WILLIAM JAMES

THE HISTORY OF
PSYCHOLOGY

The History of Psychology

By

W. B. Pillsbury, Ph.D.

Professor of Psychology, University of Michigan

NEW YORK

W·W·Norton & Company, Inc.

Publishers

Copyright, 1929

W · W · NORTON & COMPANY, INC.

70 Fifth Avenue, New York

First Edition

PRINTED IN THE UNITED STATES OF AMERICA
FOR THE PUBLISHERS BY THE VAIL-BALLOU PRESS

TABLE OF CONTENTS

ILLUSTRATIONS

PREFACE

This volume attempts to give a succinct account of the more important events in the development of psychological thinking. As philosophy and psychology are very little differentiated until the beginning of the nineteenth century, the earlier periods are given a very sketchy treatment, their bearing upon psychology being only of the most general and the personalities involved already familiar from histories of philosophy.

I have not attempted to mention every man who could be called a psychologist, but only those who have made a significant contribution to the advance of the subject by developing a theory or adding an important fact or discovering a new method. Selection will always provoke differences of opinion and no one's choice is infallible. It is especially easy to make mistakes in choosing among the lesser men, where fortunately the consequences are perhaps not so grave; but I have in every case endeavored to judge the importance of the individual from the standpoint of the value of his contribution for present-day theory rather than by the esteem of his contemporaries.

Much more space than is usual in a history of psychology has been given to the current schools; in fact,

I have had in mind a book that should give a historical setting to current controversies. This involves a certain amount of embarrassment in selection to avoid which, in part, I have been as impersonal as possible in the discussion of living men and have dealt with schools rather than with individuals. The list of current schools might be added to but I have tried to sin on the side of conservatism. As many of the doctrines discussed are still in a state of flux, the volume should be read with the date of publication in mind. It is a history and makes no attempt to indulge in prophecy. Other theories may well be born before it sees the light, and some that are mentioned here may pass into obscurity in almost as brief a time.

W. B. PILLSBURY

University of Michigan.

CHAPTER I

EARLY AND CLASSICAL GREEK PSYCHOLOGY

THE history of psychology is the story of the development of the interpretation man puts upon his acts and his thinking. Almost as soon as man began to be interested in the "why" of external objects, he also became interested in himself and in other men. This interest soon led to the development of all sorts of theories about his nature, in each of its separate aspects. A history of psychology must take the term psychology in the broadest possible meaning and must consider all the explanations that man has given of his own actions and thoughts and those of other men.

As we shall see, professed psychologists are still far from agreed as to what the specifically psychological phases of man's behaviour may be, and we cannot expect greater definiteness of the earliest thinkers. The lines between the physical and the mental, and between the mental and physiological, are very vaguely drawn. A large part of the development of the science of psychology consists in making these distinctions more definite. In a history of psychology, then, the choice of sub-

II

ject matter for each section must follow the opinion of the age with which it deals. We shall see that the early periods cover a great deal of natural science and philosophy, while the range gradually narrows as the science progresses.

From the record, it is not clear when man first began to think about himself. Most of the first writings, even, contain references to experiences that now would be called mental. Some of the earliest recorded speculations are concerned with the nature of the mind or soul. Apparently one of the first phenomena to arouse wonderment over what man really is, was death. Death meant a profound change in the life of family and comrades. The fact that the body remained while action and the possibility of communication had ceased, evoked in every race theorizing upon the possibility of the continuation of that life in another sphere. This gave rise to questions about a future existence and whether there was something that might persist after the body was dead, and if so, what it might be like. This led again to the question of how that something might be related to the body during life.

EARLY THEORIES

Very many of the early theories of the soul and of life after death were materialistic. The Egyptians, for example, assumed that the soul might re-enter the body

after death and hence were careful to preserve the body and to provide it at burial with utensils that might be used beyond the grave. Human sacrifices in Mesopotamia apparently had the purpose of supplying the dead with attendants and guards in a very physical life *after death*. Homer pictures the shades as men with all the living attributes except a physical body, and even that seems to be merely reduced to a somewhat gaseous form. Similar instances can be found in very many primitive and some present-day savage beliefs.

An attempt to explain what the soul is, or how it leaves the body at death, seems to have given rise to one of the early theories of the nature of the active or conscious principle in the body during life. Men of many different races seem to have been struck by the deep breath man draws at the moment of dying, or his heavy breathing during the final crisis of a fatal disease or injury. Possibly on a cold day the last gasp produced a definitely visible, shaped mass of moist air. Whatever may be the reason, there are in many languages evidences that breath and soul were related. In Latin *anima* is used both for breath and for soul or life. In Genesis God breathes into man's nostrils the breath of life. In all early Greek physiology, the vital processes are closely associated with air or something like it that circulates through the arteries and the nerves, when the latter are discovered by the physicians to have an important function.

THE FOUR ELEMENTS

The Greeks are usually regarded as the first to develop a specific philosophy and incidentally a psychology. It is at least true that they left the earliest written records that had an influence in the development of occidental thought. The earliest Greek thinkers had but the slightest basis for speculation. Their observations were unaided by instruments, there was an almost universal prejudice against dissection of the human body, and the study of the animal organism was very superficial and incidental. In consequence, the explanation of all phenomena was very general. We are told by Thales that everything that exists is composed of water, or something akin to it; by Heraclitus, that all is fire; by Anaximenes, that all is air. Empedocles combined all these by recognizing four elements, earth, air, fire and water, out of which the universe is compounded. These four elements persist among later thinkers, although they are sometimes reduced, as by Galen, to their most prominent qualities, the cold, the dry, the warm, and the moist. Others again used abstract principles as the basis of explanation, such as Being and Becoming, the unlimited, and *nous* or abstract Reason. Mind was explained in these terms as well as the external universe. These earliest philosophers, whose work may be traced as far back as the sixth century before

Christ, did little more than furnish a starting point, but their work was not without influence upon later men.

THE ATOMISTS

One of the schools of thinkers who were active before Socrates, began a tradition that was important throughout antiquity and has a familiar ring even at the present. This is the school of the atomists founded by Leukippos and Demokritos. They may be regarded as the forerunners of the long line of materialistic thinkers, who have changed only as advances in science make possible the assumption of new kinds of matter from which the mind may be constructed. The school derived its name from the fact that they asserted that the universe in all its parts was composed of atoms of different shapes and sizes, but otherwise alike. They are in constant motion in an empty space. Leukippos thought of these atoms as at first distributed evenly and moving irregularly, driven by no known force. In the course of chance movements, they gravitated together to constitute the masses that we know as bodies. Demokritos extended the theory to explain mind. While the body was composed of relatively large and slowly moving atoms, mind was constituted of extremely small and extremely mobile units that penetrated the interstices between the larger body atoms.

Atoms also provided the means by which objects could affect the senses, and so consciousness. The qualities of sensations were determined by the character of the atoms. In taste, for example, sourness was produced by sharp angular atoms. Hearing and sight were made possible by small particles or atoms which emanated from the luminous or sounding object and entered the sense organ, and through that penetrated to the soul within. Colors depended upon the figure of the atoms, since these would vary with the hues. The atoms thrown off by the object had forced upon them the shape of that object and thus communicated its form to the eye and so to the soul within.

DEMOKRITOS

Demokritos assigned different mental processes to different parts of the body. Thought was said to be in the brain, anger in the heart, desire in the liver. In this he was followed by Plato. He also gives a suggestion that breath may be important as an element in mind, if not its closest analogue among physical things. Each breath introduces new air into the body, serving to revivify it and even introduce new elements into the soul. We find that this atomistic theory, although crude, anticipates a fundamental idea of modern chemistry, and provides the metaphysical background for the work of the Epicureans.

The two ancient thinkers who did most to advance psychology, as well as philosophy and science in general, were Plato and Aristotle. A great number of the writings of each are preserved, and constitute the chief source of information about ancient thought. The two men were representative of different fundamental ways of approaching the development of a system of knowledge. Plato is the first great exponent of the rationalistic method. That is, he assumed certain fundamental truths and showed how others must be derived from them. Aristotle, on the other hand, was an empiricist in that he was inclined to start with a definite observation or group of observations and develop his general principles from them. This classification does only partial justice to each, for Plato made use of specific observations from time to time, and Aristotle, still more often, follows the rational method. Plato probably deserves the name rationalist more because he believed that knowledge is given in advance of specific experiences, while Aristotle gave a larger place to observation as a means of developing truth.

It should be said of both that they were hampered by the backward state of other sciences which made it difficult to find a starting point in fact for either observation or speculation. Knowledge of physics and of chemistry was of the slightest. Observations had been made of the weather and of natural phenomena, but nothing much had been accomplished in explaining them

or even in generalizing the observations. Knowledge of
the structure and function of the body was limited to
observation from without, and to studying the animals
that had been slaughtered for food. Mathematics was
relatively more advanced, but even that was confined
to counting and to what was needed for measuring land.
Geometry had been developed considerably for the latter purposes, but other branches were in a backward
state.

PLATO

Plato was born at Athens in 427 B. C. As a young
man he served as a soldier as all of his countrymen
were bound to do. When he was twenty he came under
the influence of Socrates and continued as his pupil for
some eight years. He was present at the trial of Socrates, but not at the drinking of the hemlock. His account of the trial in the Apology is one of the two important sources for that event. After Socrates' death, he
left Athens, as did most of Socrates' followers, and
studied for a time with Euclid at Megara. Later he
travelled, probably to Egypt. After that he went to
Sicily and became friendly with Dio, the brother-in-
law of the tyrant Dionysius. Through him he attempted
to influence the tyrant to introduce a more democratic
form of government. The only effect was to anger the
monarch so that he sold him into slavery in Aegina.

He was ransomed by a friend and then established himself in Athens. He founded there the famous Academy and continued to teach, with an occasional return to Sicily after the death of Dionysius, until his death in 347.

Plato's writings are mostly in the form of dialogues in which Socrates is always one of the principal speakers. It is very difficult to be sure whether he intends these remarks of Socrates to be actual reports of the theories of Socrates, or whether he uses the form for the sake of rhetorical effect. The general belief is that some are mere transcriptions of Socrates' remarks, while in most Plato himself is speaking. Most of the more analytic studies, among which are his psychological theories, are probably his own. The method makes another difficulty in that it is necessary to put together remarks scattered through various dialogues to obtain a full statement of Plato's position. He has no connected system.

Plato presented mind or soul as an active principle working to control the body, and also as the instrument for obtaining knowledge and for elaborating it into systematic form. For Plato, the soul first becomes an entity, or force, independent of the body although closely connected with it. He sometimes speaks as if it were imprisoned in the body. It is the knower, that develops or possesses knowledge, with only secondary dependence upon the sensations; it is also the source of movement and directs the acts of the body, and it is the seat, if not the source, of emotion and feeling. Plato distinguishes two stages of development in the soul, the rational and the irrational. He again divides the irrational soul into two parts, a higher and a baser. The rational soul is in the head and contains all wisdom, has clear ideas, and exerts final control. The nobler part of the irrational soul has its seat in the heart, is the bearer of the nobler impulses and emotions, including courage. The baser part of the irrational soul, the source of the appetites and lower passions, has its seat below the diaphragm. The assignment of seats seems to have been determined for superficial reasons. The highest soul was put in the head because it was nearest heaven. The irrational soul was given the local habitat for each of its parts on the basis of the sensations that accompany the activity of each. Plato observed movements in the body during the emotional responses and assigned the corresponding part of the body as the seat of the part of the soul responsible for them.

It is to the problem of knowledge that Plato makes the most important contribution. Knowledge appears to originate in the senses, which must obviously make certain contributions; but nevertheless, if derived altogether from the senses, it would have no high degree of certainty. In consequence, Plato regards part of knowledge as dependent upon sensation, and part as due to the ideas that are in the mind from the beginning. The sense organs are affected by movements in the air

and surrounding media in general, and through them
give a notion of the nature of objects. The sense organs
are easily moved. In some senses there is motion in the
organ in advance of sensation which makes the organ
more susceptible to the stimulus. This is particularly
true of the eye. Plato assumes that there is light or fire
in the eye that goes forth to meet the light coming from
the object. The presence of fire in the eye is inferred
from the reflection that can be seen on the cornea and
from the lens. Sight takes place when the fire within joins
the fire from without. For Plato, motion replaces the
atoms of the atomists. Otherwise the principles of sensation are similar.

The most characteristic and lasting contribution that
Plato made to the theory of knowledge is that sensations do not themselves suffice, but must before they
give true knowledge be supplemented and corrected
by the ideas innate in the soul. For Plato, ideas are the
prototypes of things, that exist before objects in the
universe or in the mind of God and are part of the original endowment of the soul before any experience. When
the soul enters the body, the ideas may be in some degree contaminated, so that even they do not contain absolutely perfect knowledge. Still they constitute the
nearest approach that man can make to truth. When a
sensation is received, it arouses the corresponding idea,
and the two interact. The formal and more perfect truth
comes from the idea, the sensation is the temporary oc-

casion. It is difficult to assign the separate functions to each part. Plato is not quite clear on the point, and it would be difficult to develop an altogether consistent theory of knowledge from his notion. In general, sensation provides the occasion for knowledge and new data, that comes through immediate contact with the external world. Ideas give generality and so raise thought and perception above the merely temporary and transient. Error is due in part to the contamination of the soul by the body, and in part to a misinterpretation of sensations.

An element in Plato's theory of knowledge, related to the assumption that ideas come into the body with the soul, was the belief that certain experiences might be retained from an earlier existence. This Plato probably took over from the mystic Orphic tradition that assumed the transmigration of souls. Now and again an experience seems to be familiar though we can connect it with no event in our past. Plato would explain this familiarity as the result of having lived through the event in some earlier incarnation in another being. He called the phenomenon reminiscence. It is of interest primarily in showing the mixture in Plato of naive credulity with the greatest intellectual keenness.

Plato makes several empirical observations on memory and the course of ideas. Memory is the mere persistence or preservation of a sensation. Any sensation that really enters the soul is never lost, although many sense impressions leave no effect because they never reach the soul. An idea may be actual or potential. Most ideas persist as actually conscious processes. When they lapse into forgetfulness, they are merely overlooked and may be rearoused by active effort. Plato also noticed that older connections are a factor in the arousal of ideas. In the Phaedo he remarks that a lyre may rearouse the memory of the player of the instrument, or of his friend. This would be the modern association by contiguity. He recognized too that like may recall like, our modern association by similarity.

The feelings and emotions receive less recognition in Plato's writings than the intellectual processes. All sensation is movement, as has been said, and when the movement becomes violent, emotion arises. If the movement is natural, pleasure is aroused; if unnatural, pain. Emotions and passions are also ascribed to the movements of the lower abdomen. Feelings and emotions really are inherent in the soul rather than in the body, for the body has no consciousness. Discussed abstractly as a function of the soul, desire is said to be due to a lack, which is in itself painful and which is accompanied by a thought of the perfect state that would supplant it. Volition grows out of the appreciation of the lack, and of the change necessary to alleviate the resulting emotion. The soul enters a neutral state when the desire is satisfied. In his more practical treatises on education and politics, Plato makes the appreciation of the end or purpose dominate man in his conduct. While Plato receives most attention for his doctrine of ideas and explanation of knowledge, he had a theory of action, even if action was subordinated to desire and so to feeling.

ARISTOTLE

Of all the Greeks, Aristotle exerted the greatest influence upon the course of the world's thought. Uncertain as are all universal statements, one might fairly safely venture the estimate that he has influenced the thought of the world more than any other man who has ever lived. Many of his writings were preserved and became the accepted standards in philosophy and science, not only through antiquity but in the church schools of the later Middle Ages. They then served as a point of departure for the revival of learning in modern times, and even now, they are explicitly and knowingly revived from time to time, and many a theory, propounded as new, proves to be merely a doctrine of Aristotle presented in slightly modified form.

Aristotle was born in Stagira in Asia Minor, in the year 384 B. C. On the early death of his father, who had been physician to Amytas of Macedon, grandfather of Alexander the Great, Aristotle returned to his native Stagira, leaving again at the age of seventeen to become a student of Plato in the Academy at Athens.

He continued as a student for twenty years, until Plato's death. The Academy was constituted of a group of scholars who recognized Plato as master and lived together under his general direction. The organization was informal and took the name from the place in the suburbs of Athens where they met. At first, they merely attended the lectures and discussions conducted by Plato. As they became more mature, they acted as tutors for the younger students, and themselves gave lectures. Aristotle began his teaching with rhetoric. At the death of Plato, he withdrew to Assos in Mysia. When this city was conquered by the Persians, he fled to Mytilene on the island of Lesbos. Later he was summoned to the court of Philip and made tutor to the young Alexander. The school was established in the small town of Mieza, near a stalactite cave at the foot of a mountain. This duty continued for only two years. After that Aristotle returned to Athens and drew together a school of his own. It was for this school that he prepared most of the discourses constituting the works that have come down to us. Alexander's death was followed by a hostile outbreak against his old tutor, and Aristotle fled to Chalcis in the Island of Euboea, where he died in 322 B. C.

Aristotle is important for the development of psychology both because of his theories and because of his acute observations of specific facts. While for Plato the soul was a distinct entity and seems to have come into the body at birth, for Aristotle mind was rather a way of responding, a function rather than a thing. Mind is closely related to life. He recognizes three levels of complexity in the functioning of a living being. The lowest is the nutritive, the second in complexity is the appetitive function, and the highest is the rational or thinking function. Each of these ways of functioning he calls a soul. He sometimes calls the first, the plant soul; the second, the animal soul; and the third, the human or rational soul. The exact relation of these souls to the body is not always clear, and probably varies somewhat from passage to passage. They are always apparently connected with the body and there is always a mutual relation between them, although the soul is the dominant factor, and sometimes is made a directing force. In one passage Aristotle speaks of the nutritive soul as related to the body as cutting is related to the knife. In other places he speaks as if the nutritive soul exercised certain directive functions in the vital processes. In this sense, it became the prototype of the modern notion of vitalism, as when Johannes Müller introduces a "vital force," that marks the difference between living and dead matter and is assumed to direct the life processes in a way not possible of explanation by physical and chemical action.

Similarly, the highest soul is spoken of as the *entelechy* of the body, a word which may be mentioned because it has been frequently used by recent writers. For Aristotle it seems to imply again a relation between the

soul and body in which the soul leads in determining
the course of action and thought and at the same time
is organically one with the body. Now the directing,
now the functional unity and interdependence is emphasized. Aristotle also tried to make his notion clear by
the statement that the soul was the form, the body the
matter. Without form, matter has no meaning, but the
form is not apart from the matter, is probably not necessarily before the matter, and would also be impossible without it. The two are together; each is necessary to the existence of the other. While the form must
be given the leading part, it does not control matter.
These analogies still offer useful ways of thinking of
the relation of mind and body, and have been used by
current writers.

Aristotle's knowledge of the human body was su-
perior to Plato's in spite of the fact that he puts the rational soul in the heart instead of in the brain as modern
knowledge does. The heart dominates the body, both as
a directing force and as the source of heat. The food
that is taken into the stomach is there distilled to become *ichor*, the nutritive substance, which rises to the
heart. By further distillation, under the influence of the
heat in the heart, it becomes blood and circulates
through the body. By a further refinement animal spirits, also called the connatural spirits, are derived from
the blood. These seem to circulate through the arteries
and are the source of sensation and the means of direct-

ing movement. It should be emphasized that nothing was known of the different functions of arteries, nerves and even tendons. Blood was assumed to move through the veins, for these were seen to be filled with blood when an animal was examined after death. The arteries are empty at death and so were assumed to be the pathways by which the animal spirits passed. The nerves and even the tendons were sometimes confused with the arteries in this function.

The function of the *pneuma*, which we have called animal spirits, a term usually applied by later writers, is a puzzle not only in Aristotle but in most of the ancient and medieval writers, and even as late as Descartes. It is said to be derived in part from the blood and in part from the outer air. Different writers assign to it characteristics ranging from those of mechanically driven air, to those of more or less animate messengers that make deliberate movements. In theory it is always rather mechanical than conscious, but practical use tended to give it human characteristics. The pneuma for Aristotle was the medium of communication between the senses and the heart, the center of consciousness. It was also the medium through which the soul in the heart transmitted impulses to the muscles and tendons and so produced movements.

While for Plato knowledge is little more than the reawakening of ideas contained in the soul from before birth, for Aristotle the sensations furnish the real ma-

terials of knowledge. All sensations are aroused by something in the objects, which acts upon a medium, and this in turn communicates a motion to the sense organ. Hearing arises when motion of the sounding body is communicated to the air, the medium of sound, and through it affects the ear. Color in the object affects the *diaphanous*, a medium extended through the universe, and this carries the effect to the eye. Smell has a similar peculiar medium which is contained in both air and water, for fishes smell, and there is no air in water. For taste and touch the medium is the flesh on the outer body of the sensing organ, the tongue for taste and the skin for touch. In addition to this mechanical explanation of the stimulation of the senses through motion, Aristotle has a more metaphysical theory. He asserts that each object is like man in that it has both form and matter, and the "form" or essence may leave the matter of the object in an immaterial way and come through the sense to the pure "form" of the body and there be perceived. In this case pure essence in the object appeals directly to the pure form of the body, the mind.

Aristotle introduces a stage in knowing intermediate between the single senses and the soul, the "common sense." Its seat is in the heart and its function is to coordinate the contributions of the different senses. When gaps are present in the material offered by the special senses, or when there is contradiction between them, the common sense fills in the gaps and harmonizes the inconsistencies. The common sense also perceives the properties that can be supplied by no single sense, such as motion, rest, form, number, and magnitude. After common sense has done its part, the active reason completes the interpretation. It uses the materials of the senses, special and common, and makes the final synthesis. This adds the completing touch to fully rational knowledge.

In addition to the theoretical discussion of the development of knowledge, Aristotle makes several shrewd empirical observations on the course of mental processes, especially of memory and imagination. Memory always involves an image, and thus is to be regarded as the reinstatement after a lapse of time of a sensory process. He also notices that recall is through suggestion and enumerates at least three of the four laws of association that were recognized by the later writers. His description of the process of recall is vivid.[1] "When, therefore, we recollect, we awaken certain antecedent processes and continue this until we call up that particular experience, after which the desired one is wont to appear. That is the reason why we hunt through a series in thought, beginning with an object presently before us, or with something else, or with an object that is similar or opposite or contiguous. In this way recognition is awakened." This is the first clear description of our way of recalling or imagining.

[1] De Memoria, 451b, Hammond's translation, page 205.

Affective life and action receive less consideration and are on the whole subordinated to knowledge. Action occurs on the occasion of sensation, and with the active coöperation of reason. Physiologically, the pneuma carries the sensory impression from the sense organ to the heart, and there a second impulse of the pneuma is started by the sensation which goes forth from the heart to the muscle and causes that to move the member. All this is under the control of reason.

Pleasure and pain also arise in connection with sensation. Each sensation is accompanied by pleasure or pain. Pleasure comes with a free activity, displeasure when activity is checked. Emotions are said to arise when there is a mixture of both qualities, which are sometimes predominantly pleasurable, again are predominantly unpleasant. Aristotle gives a careful analysis of several concrete emotions, among them anger, hate, fear, courage, envy, and joy. More abstract is his theory of the relation of desire to action. Desire always arises from a felt pain or lack, since this awakens at once the thought of the satisfaction of the deficiency or removal of the pain. Action follows upon this realization. Conation is thus controlled by the affective life. On the other hand, both are related to the intellectual life, since man desires that which he thinks to be good. What he shall think to be good depends upon his appreciation and knowledge, and upon his rational interpretation of a situation. The whole life, affective and volitional, is

CHAPTER II

LATER GREEK AND MEDIEVAL PSYCHOLOGY

THE later Greek schools of philosophy offered little of value to psychology. Stoicism and Epicureanism were primarily interested in ethics, and psychology took a minor place in their writings.

THE STOICS

The Stoics had as their guiding principle the ideal of escaping from the control of the emotions. The soul of man is related to the pneuma of Aristotle. It is thought of as something between breath and fire that pervades all parts of the body and is also closely related to, if not one in principle with, the world soul. In its function it is identical with reason, and makes possible consistent intelligent action. Emotions are the outcome of chance impulses and uncertainly determined movements that originate in the senses and in the lower bodies. They are excessive or unnatural movements of the soul. True virtue comes with perfect knowledge and the subordination of these erratic movements of the emotions to the calm

ST. AUGUSTINE

We may mention the contributions of two men as representative of this long period. St. Augustine, the monk and hermit of Hippo, 354–450, was typical of the first period, and was the recognized leader of thought in the Church during the succeeding six centuries. He combined certain strains of the Greek tradition with the Hebrew and Pauline psychology of the Christian doctrine. St. Augustine was born in North Africa in 354 of a Christian mother and pagan father. At first he was a follower of the Manichaean sect. When thirty-three he embraced the Christian religion, and progressing slowly in his belief in the doctrine finally became a leader of the Church, and later was made Bishop of Hippo in North Africa. In his confessions he tells of his life, incidentally of his psychological and more specifically of his theological beliefs. Something of both can also be found in his *de Civitate Dei*.

A mixture of philosopher and mystic seer, of rationalist and ecstatic, he formulated the psychology that dominated the church doctrines for some five or six centuries. He took much of the Platonic soul doctrine from the later Platonists. The soul for him is independent but closely related to the body. It was created by God at the same time as the body and controls man's acts in every way. The soul is intimately associated with all the life processes and permeates all parts of the body, but seems to be most intimately connected with the brain. The brain receives impressions from the senses and sends out motor impulses to the muscles everywhere. The resulting movements are not spontaneous as in reflex acts, but are directed closely by the soul. He gives a detailed discussion of memory, which he regards as an immediate function of the soul and not to be thought of as a storehouse. He recognizes Aristotle's common sense as the mediator between the separate senses and the soul, since it makes the preliminary coördination of the sense data.

In Augustine is found the first definite development of the faculty psychology that constitutes so large a part of popular psychology of all times. Memory, imagination, and will are among the more important of the faculties. Of these the dominant place is given to the will. As exhibited in attention, will selects from among the objects offered by sense a few to become conscious. It also controls remembering, but in the light of the dictates of reason. Imagination again is intermediate in function between memory and reason. It must use the materials of sense that have been retained by memory, but has certain of the independent capacities of reason. From this it will be seen that the faculties are regarded as partially independent capacities. Probably in most cases there is intended something of a human analogy. Each faculty stands to the others much as one man in a partnership, with a par-

tially independent voice but bound by the final decisions of the whole group. It is a remnant of the tendency to look at all forces after the pattern of man, the
so-called anthropomorphic tendency that runs through
all primitive thought and is only partially superseded
in the most scientific. For Augustine each of these faculties is a part of the unitary soul, but a part that still
preserves a considerable measure of independence. St.
Augustine does not present a definite system of psychology, but scatters his contributions through his
works, written to develop a system of theology, and to
advance the Christian religion. His psychology is important because of its influence in later theological discussions, and because through its adoption by the
church, it became widely popular, and is still current
as the psychology of the man in the street.

THE TWELFTH CENTURY

The period from Augustine to the twelfth century was
truly the dark age for psychology, as for most of
science and philosophy. This was primarily a time when
thinking was discouraged, for man had little leisure left
from political conflicts and from meeting the neces-
sities of existence. So far as there was any psychology,
Augustine's doctrines persisted. There was no incentive
for independent thought, and the church did not encourage it, even when occasion arose. The classical

schools were forgotten, and many of the works were actually destroyed lest they weaken Christian belief. The Arabs had preserved the writings of Aristotle, after the destruction of the library at Alexandria, and continued to write commentaries on them. By contacts with Spain, their influence spread in some degree throughout Europe and when the Moors were driven from Spain, copies of the works of Aristotle became available to European scholars. After this came obscure stirrings of interest in scientific and philosophical thought.

We may regard the twelfth century as marking the humble beginnings of a revival, even if that revival was largely no more than a renewed knowledge of Aristotle, with mild reactions upon his teachings. The men who deserve most credit in this movement were Albert the Great (1193–1280) and Thomas Aquinas. They did much to extend the doctrines of Aristotle and to modify them to the uses of the Church. A little later, but still contemporary with them, Roger Bacon (1215?–1292?) in England was asserting the claims of the empirical method, which was later to make science possible. His influence was more general than specific. Of the two saints, Albert is regarded, as on the whole, the more original, although Thomas, his pupil and collaborator, left a greater mark on the history of psychology and philosophy because of his power of systematization. His works became the accepted doctrines of the Catholic Church and still stand as the basis of the Church psychology. We may briefly summarize his system as typical of the age.

THOMAS AQUINAS

Thomas in his life illustrates the peculiarly international character of the knowledge and teaching of that period. He was born at Rocassica in the Kingdom of Naples, in 1225 or 1227, and when he entered the priesthood became a pupil of Albert at Cologne. He continued his studies at Paris. There it is said, he was refused a degree because of jealousy on the part of the authorities. Later, after he had become a distinguished authority, he came back and was given his degree together with other honors and amid popular acclaim. This cosmopolitanism of knowledge was made possible in the middle ages primarily because Latin was the language of the church, and all lecturing and writing was in a language common to the learned of all lands. St. Thomas, an Italian by birth, was as much at home in the brotherhood at Cologne as he would have been at Rome, and he could transfer his studies or his lecturing to Paris with no necessity of learning a new language.

The contribution St. Thomas made consisted in a modification of Aristotle's ideas to fit the needs of the age, primarily to make them harmonize with the prevailing doctrine of Augustine. The notion of the soul in the form given it by Paul and the church fathers must be modified to agree with the "form" of Aristotle. "Form," it will be remembered, was for Aristotle the determiner of matter, but it was not a force or thing apart, nor was it self-determined. It was an essential part of matter and subject to impersonal laws. Thomas identified it with the soul of Augustine, which made it a personal force, and the active determiner of the body's actions. It ceased to be a part of the living whole, an ingenious way of representing one phase of a living individual, and became a humanized being, that acted on its own volition, and was capable of no further analysis or explanation. He also made it survive the body at death, a point that was vital for the Christian religion but had been left very uncertain by Aristotle himself.

Knowledge was, for Thomas, in part derived from sensation, in part dependent upon the soul, which either developed it from itself or recognized immediate innate truths. He followed Aristotle in accepting a hierarchy of processes in perception. The senses furnished the first crude materials. These were coördinated by the common sense which gave them certain of their general characteristics, including extent and duration. Then reason imparted to them the seal of final truth by stamping upon them the universal form. Thomas emphasized Aristotle's direct sensing of the "form" as opposed to the matter of an object. The form or intelligible "species" may be freed from the matter of the object and

come through the senses to the soul. These forms are
the primary source of knowledge, and mediate between
the object and the form of the individual, the soul.
"Form" speaks directly to "form."

In addition to the intellectual processes, Thomas discusses the appetitive and voluntary functions, emotions
and will. Both were subordinated to the intellect. Emotions were likely to disturb pure thought when given
full sway but might and should be controlled. The will
was dominated by the intellect, for one must always
seek that which reason proves to be best. But this necessity which depends upon internal causes is still true
freedom, a freedom to seek that which is shown to be
best. St. Thomas, like St. Augustine, was definitely
devoted to a faculty system of psychology. It must be
said that he showed great acuteness in analysis, but
contributes little or nothing from concrete observation.
The system as a whole merits mention because it was
typical of later medieval thought, and because of its
later influence, rather than because it itself makes any
real advance upon the systems of earlier writers.

CHAPTER III

THE BEGINNINGS OF MODERN PSYCHOLOGY
DESCARTES AND SPINOZA

THE first awakening of a modern attitude towards philosophical and to a less degree towards psychological problems is usually dated from Descartes. The passing from the medieval towards the modern spirit was gradual. Many of the church men in the scholastic period would become aware of the advantages of investigation on some one point, but their contributions were not followed up and were apparently lost. The sixteenth century saw the beginning of enlightenment in many fields. The religious reformers had already asserted the right to free thought against old dogma or current authority, which could be carried over to justification of doubt of the statements of Aristotle, Thomas, or Galen, in psychological as well as in religious matters. The voyages to America had been in part the result of scientific discoveries, especially the invention of the compass, as well as of the general spirit of adventure carried over from the realm of thought to actual voyaging. The discovery of the New World widened the intellectual as well as the geographical boundaries of Europe, for it brought new contacts, new wealth, and justified the spirit of daring in thought as well as in physical ventures.

For a century or more there had been advances in science in several lands. Vesalius, Sylvius, and Servetus had made contributions to anatomy; Harvey had demonstrated the circulation of the blood, a fact which although not recognized in all its implications, began a complete transformation of many related notions; Leonardo had made investigations in many fields of science; Kepler, Galileo, and Bacon, all contemporaries of Descartes, show the effect of the general intellectual awakening, in astronomy, physics, and general scientific theory. All this indicates that the bonds of old authority had been broken and man was more willing to think for himself.

DESCARTES

Descartes was born at La Haye in Touraine, in 1596. He came of a wealthy family of the lesser nobility, and as a younger son his father prepared him for a career as a soldier. Entered at the Jesuit school at La Flèche, he acquired facility in the ancient languages and studied what science was offered in the school. Of the sciences, only mathematics made much impression upon him as all else seemed too uncertain or too trivial. When he left school, Descartes did not enter at once upon his career, because he was somewhat feeble of body, but spent seven years in Paris, exercising physically to increase his strength and studying for his own pleasure. He found that his friends provided too much of a distraction from serious work, so partly to escape them, partly to further the design of becoming a soldier, and partly to broaden his outlook, he went to Holland in 1619 and entered the army of the Prince of Orange. Later he served in the Bavarian army and also under the flag of the Hapsburg Emperor of Germany. His military life apparently was never taken very seriously, and was regarded more as an adventure for the sake of learning the world, than as a real career. So it seems that Descartes took some part in the campaigns of the first two years of the Thirty Years War but was never in actual battle. It was a period of contemplation and observation. In 1624, he concluded his travels by a two-year sojourn in Rome, from 1624–26, and then returned to Paris with the intention of settling down to complete several works of a philosophical and mathematical nature that had been begun in the intervals of his travels.

This intention was postponed, first by his taking part in the siege of La Rochelle, and again when he settled in Paris once more after this interruption. Discovering anew that his friends were too distracting, he returned to the Netherlands, and lived for twenty years in Amsterdam, Utrecht and Leyden. In 1649 he was invited by

Queen Christine to live in Stockholm and give her lessons. He accepted and wrote his work on the Emotions *(Les Passions de l'Ame)* at her suggestion. He found the climate and the teaching made severe demands upon him, especially as the Queen set the daily lesson at five in the morning. His death in 1650 was ascribed to the great strain of this life.

Descartes wrote works on mathematics—he is considered the founder of analytic geometry—on physical optics, and on philosophy. In psychology he is important for developing a theory of the relation between body and mind and for his analysis of the emotions. His method of establishing the truth of a proposition is interesting psychologically, since it rests upon a quality of mental processes. His assumption is that any proposition is true if it can be thought clearly and distinctly. By this method he convinces himself of the existence of God. He reaches a belief in the existence of himself, which he interprets as the soul, by an equally direct and famous process. He asserts that he is certain that he thinks, therefore he, the thinker, must exist. *Cogito ergo sum.* Should one doubt this or any other proposition, the conclusion is the same. The very fact of doubting proves the existence of the doubter. *Dubito ergo sum.*

His most important contribution to psychology was the development of a notion of the relation between body and mind. This is a philosophical problem but it is also the foundation of psychology. Descartes initiated a series of theories that cover most of the possible ways of thinking about the relation of body and mind. Before him all thinkers had regarded the two as in some way phases of the same whole, although they separated the phases in different degrees. Descartes made mind and body absolutely distinct in kind and in the laws that must be applied to them. Mind is defined as the thinking substance, body as the extended substance. Mind and matter are for the first time made subject to absolutely different laws. It may be said that Descartes, like a small boy with a mechanical puzzle, had taken the two apart and that philosophers ever since have been trying to fit them together again, so far with only indifferent success.

While Descartes defined the body as the extended substance he worked out in great detail the more important mechanisms and explained all functions on the principles of mechanics. He had the advantage of the discoveries of the preceding centuries—especially he knew of the circulation of the blood through Harvey's work; nevertheless, his treatment strikes one rather for its similarities to than for its differences from Galen's work. The seat of intelligence is in the brain and the animal spirits provide the means by which the brain is acted upon by the senses, and through which it exerts an effect upon the muscles. The animal spirits are gaseous in nature and are derived from the blood by a process of distillation. The moving force in the body is the heat produced in the heart from the food. Through its action primarily the blood is kept in circulation. The blood itself is derived by a process of filtration and distillation from the food taken into the stomach. The particles of food that are sufficiently fine pass through the walls of the stomach and rise to the heart. From the heart one larger artery goes to the brain and the animal spirits are derived from the blood in much the same way that the blood is derived from the food. Only the finest particles can pass through the very fine openings into the brain and these constitute the animal spirits. While the picture of bodily action is crude, it is important in that everything is referred to purely physical principles and the spiritual forces of the ancients are eliminated entirely. The body is merely a machine.

The mind, although defined as the thinking substance, is still definite enough to be given a specific seat. Purely theoretical considerations led to the choice of the organ with which it was to be connected. The mind is unitary and hence must have a single organ. Descartes could find in the brain but one such, the pineal body on the roof of the third ventricle in the midbrain. This was also near enough the center of the brain to meet the requirement of ready accessibility. It is somewhat spherical in shape and placed on the end of rather a long and flexible stalk. We now know that it has no nervous function, but is one of the so-called ductless glands that secretes a substance essential to the growth of parts of the body. According to Descartes, the mind sits in this organ and is moved by the animal spirits, and may also move the animal spirits when occasion requires. When one sees, a movement is started in the eye that drives the animal spirits inward over the optic nerve to the third ventricle; this inclines the pineal gland and produces in the mind a picture of the object. On the other hand when the mind desires to move a member it can direct the animal spirits to the proper muscles and they produce the movement. Thus body acts on mind and mind acts on body directly. This form of relation of mind and body is what we have come to call interactionism.

Descartes ascribes ideas partly to the body and partly to the soul. The very clear ideas and those that give the most fundamental truths are innate in the soul, such as the idea of God, of the self, and the axioms of mathematics. The ideas of external objects come through the senses, others, like hunger and thirst and awareness of the emotions, arise within the body and affect the mind. We must also recognize ideas of an intermediate type in which the innate ideas and ideas derived from the senses combine. On the whole, however, he speaks as if ideas were in the mind alone, and makes no attempt to find a counterpart of them in the brain. In a few passages he does depart from this and speaks as if memories were connected with traces left on the brain. In one place, he describes the animal spirits as running through the pores of the brain until they find the specific memories desired by the mind.

Descartes made relatively few attempts to formulate specific laws of mental action. Some of the more interesting deal with the emotions and are discussed in *Les Passions de l'Ame*. Emotions arise when the animal spirits are too greatly agitated. This depends in part upon the heat in the heart and in part upon the character of the fluids that arise from the stomach. Agitation of the animal spirits in the brain has as its first effect the sending of the spirits back to the heart to increase the openings into that organ, which increases the flow of blood to the brain. At the same time the animal spirits move the pineal gland and so communicate the effect to the soul. The real seat of the emotions is in the body. Were there not a body in connection with the soul there would be no emotions. Within limits, the mind can influence the emotions, but only by imagining situations that are suited to arouse or check them. Descartes speaks as if the emotions were indicative of probable benefit or injury to the body and are aroused before the mind knows that the object is useful or injurious, an early suggestion of the notion of instinct.

Descartes has six primary emotions: admiration (wonder), love, hate, desire, joy, and sadness. Wonder or admiration is the most intellectual and so belongs more to the soul and less to the body. "It is a sudden surprise of our soul which causes it to consider with attention that which to it appears infrequent and extraordinary." The other emotions are given a more mechanical explanation. Each may originate in some association between an external object and movements of the body that were connected with it. These movements may favor or impede the action of the body and cause animal spirits to rise to the brain. "In love one feels a sweet warmth in the chest, and that the digestion of food goes on more quickly, so that this emotion is useful to the health." While the emotions are due primarily to the physical changes in the body, he also recognizes the influence of old associations. When one sees an object that has previously been present at the time an emotion has been experienced, it will induce that emotion, even if it were not itself of a character to arouse the emotion. This may be said to be the first recognition of a conditioned reaction. Descartes gives the most complete outline of all psychological details in *Les Passions de l'Ame*, from which we have been quoting.

Descartes also had an important influence upon later thought by his complete separation of animal and man. Animals are denied souls and so are reduced to mere machines. This led later writers, especially the materialists, to raise the question why man also might not be understood purely from mechanical principles and why a soul was necessary to explain anything at all. Descartes had no notion of reducing the mind to a smaller place in his explanation than the theologians, although even in his lifetime the influence of his teachings upon orthodoxy was questioned. Once at Utrecht he was summoned before the church authorities, but he refused to heed the summons and was protected by the protest of the French ambassador. Later, at Leyden, the protestant ministers accused him before the curators of the University, but he was acquitted of atheism after some delay. Descartes had no desire to come into conflict with the church, as is shown by his withholding an astronomical treatise from publication after he learned of the condemnation of Galileo.

GEULINCX

Descartes affected thought immediately by setting the problem of the relation of body and mind rather than by his concrete psychological theories and observations. In France a number of men tried to improve his picture of the way body and mind interact. Geulincx, (1625–1669) one of the first, eliminated interactionism almost altogether by assuming that God acted as the really efficient cause whenever a physical event seemed to cause an idea or an idea was followed by a movement. The series of physical events followed a course demanded by physical laws, and the mental events followed their own course. Whenever a physical event occurred, God intervened to initiate in the minds of all the beholders an idea that corresponded to that event.

In the same way, whenever a man's mind developed an intention of moving a member, God stepped in and moved the member in the way desired. This doctrine is known as occasionalism, for the event in either series is only the occasion that suggests to the deity that it is time for the corresponding event to appear in the other series.

MALEBRANCHE

More generally important, although not much more adequate in his explanation of this particular process, was Malebranche (1638–1715), who held that God produced the ideas in the mind without any necessary reference to events in the outside world. The object did not always have the form of the idea, although usually the idea represents a true object. The ideas are modified by the connections in which they are seen. All things are relative. Malebranche was interested in the illusion of the moon appearing to be greater on the horizon than at the zenith and uses the notion of its relation to objects seen against it as the explanation. He also noted the laws of recall through association, made experiments on after-images, and gave much time to the laws of the refraction of light and other optical phenomena. His results are a curious mixture of careful observation and mystical interpretation. He always comes back to the fundamental notion that both mental and physical phe-

nomena are directly due to the acts of God, although he does much to trace the empirical laws of connection in both fields. God manages to keep the two series in step although there is no causal connection between them.

SPINOZA

The most important follower of Descartes, although possibly a follower in time rather more than in ideas, was Benedict Baruch Spinoza. Spinoza was also a refugee in Holland, although of a very different character and for a very different reason. Spinoza's family was driven to Holland by the persecutions of the Jews in Portugal, while Descartes went there to escape the too pleasant company of convivial friends. Spinoza was always poor and lived in obscurity, while Descartes came of a well to do and distinguished family.

Spinoza was born in Amsterdam in 1632. Educated first in the rabbinical school, he later came under the influence of a Dutch teacher, from whom he learned the languages. He became acquainted early with the writings of Descartes and was sufficiently influenced by them to find himself unable to accept the religious teachings of his people. He broke completely with his synagogue, was abandoned by his friends, and lived most of his life under suspicion by both Jew and gentile. Realizing early that some means of support other than his writing was necessary, he apprenticed himself to a lens grinder and lived by that trade until his death. The calling fitted well with his interest in optics, although it provided only a meager return. He was proudly independent and so devoted to his thinking that he even declined a call to the University of Heidelberg, lest his time be broken in upon by teaching and disputation. Spinoza died at the Hague in 1677.

Spinoza also is most important for psychology through his theory of the relation of body and mind, and for his discussion of emotions. In a sense he attempted to revive the ancient view of the mind-body relation by making both different phases of the same substance. Descartes had succeeded in making them so completely separate that he could not assert that they were related as form and matter, or as two different kinds of matter. Instead Spinoza insisted that they were really different aspects of a single substance. The thinker himself appreciates this substance as idea or consciousness, the outside observer sees the same substance, so far as he appreciates it at all, as body. This is known as the double aspect theory of the relation of body and mind and has followers to this day. There is really but one series of events and so only one cause for any phenomenon. The common substance which presents itself under this twofold aspect Spinoza identified with God. God is the true reality and presents himself in these two fundamentally distinct ways. On this view, mental states do not affect bodily processes, nor do physical processes produce changes in mental states. All changes occur in the one real substance and are the expression of the antecedent conditions of the divine being. The theory makes impossible any freedom of the individual, because man is part of the universal whole, and his life, in thought and action, is but a fragment of the divine substance.

What of detailed psychology can be found in Spinoza's works is given in the *Ethics*. This is an attempt to deduce all truth from a few simple axioms, following the rigid method and forms of geometry. As a style it is cumbersome, and the logic did not follow the geometrical demonstration. In his treatment of mental states Spinoza distinguished degrees of clearness. The clearest are derived from pure reason and are to be absolutely trusted. Certain intermediate ones come through the senses and may be aided to clearness by reason. Still others arise in the body alone, are very uncertain, and constitute the emotions. The object of life should be to progress from the unclear states to the certainty and clearness of reason. This complete clearness also gives the nearest approximation to freedom that man can attain to.

Dynamically, emotions are pictured as a struggle of the individual towards self-protection or self-realization. When man is struggling vainly and with little clear knowledge of direction he suffers pain and has only vague ideas. These are the unpleasant emotions. When he is moving towards a goal, he has pleasure. There is thus a distinction between the pleasantness or unpleasantness of mental states which corresponds to success or failure in attaining the end of life. Alongside of this is the distinction of clearness, which assumes that the appetites are unclear because they depend upon the body alone, and that mental states increase in clearness as they are more and more derived from pure reason.

Spinoza gives a detailed discussion and explanation of the separate emotions. He has three primary emotions, joy, sadness and desire. Joy corresponds to bodily well-being and progress towards an end; sadness to bodily ill-being or to being thwarted in progress. Desire adds to the others a slightly conscious awareness of seeking an end. All the other emotions are derived from these by the addition of different ideas. Thus hate is defined as sadness with the idea of the external cause; inclination is joy accompanied by the idea of the object assumed to be the cause of the joy. In his explanation he recognizes the laws of association that may transfer an emotion from its first cause to another through simultaneous action. Some of this classification is formal, other parts are full of shrewd observation even from the modern standpoint. Thus Spinoza gave a more subtle picture of the relation of mind and body than any of his predecessors, also working out certain of the detailed applications of his theory.

CHAPTER IV

ENGLISH PSYCHOLOGY AND LEIBNIZ'S RE-
ACTION AGAINST IT: HOBBES, LOCKE,
AND LEIBNIZ

A S opposed to the rational character of the continental thinkers, we find across the channel an almost universal tendency to follow an inductive or empirical method. Descartes was willing to break with
the scholastic philosophy and did so almost completely.
He nevertheless used the method of the syllogism after
he had carefully investigated his general principles.
The English school on the contrary holds close to direct
observation of the facts of mind. It is also characteristi-
cally little interested in the ultimate nature of objects
or of mind, and when it ventures a theory of the real
essence of these substances, it does not seem to take
them quite seriously. They may be abandoned or
changed without too great consideration for consistency.
This is true even in Hobbes, who advocates the use of
the deductive method of mathematics and has little respect for Bacon or his inductive approach.

The inductive spirit of the British thinker was not
a matter of late growth. We find it in the old church-
men, John of Salisbury and Roger Bacon, as well as in

Francis Bacon and the later philosophers. To psychology this brings an entirely new flavor. The material is to be found in an observation of mental states or processes, considered as if they were real things. They are taken for granted, described, the order of their appearance and disappearance is traced, and they are related to the phenomena of the objective sciences for their explanation. While Descartes and Spinoza are interested in speculating as to how body and mind may be defined, and how they may be related to God, Hobbes, Locke and their English successors ask how ideas are aroused, how sensations develop. They show slight tendency to speculate on questions far removed from observation and when they do speculate, they refer the observed facts to causes of a mechanical kind. There is a progressive scepticism about the similarity of objects without to their mental counterparts in mind as we go on from Hobbes to Hume. Hobbes barely questions the similarity. Locke accepts certain of the senses as giving real knowledge and denies that correspondence to others. Berkeley and Hume abandon all assumptions as to the nature of external things and even deny the existence of them.

HOBBES

Thomas Hobbes stands in a somewhat unique relation to Descartes and to Locke. He was born before Descartes, and yet did not die until twenty years after him. He knew of Descartes' work but had little respect for it and seems to have been little influenced by it. He lived before Locke, but seems to have had slight effect upon him. Their attitudes had much in common, but the similarities were due to temperament and not, apparently, to direct borrowing. Hobbes was born in Malmesbury in 1588, prematurely, he said, because his mother was afraid of the approaching Spanish Armada. As a believer in maternal influence he ascribed his timorous nature to the emotional attitude of his mother at the time of his birth. His father struck a priest when Hobbes was still an infant and left the region to return no more. His mother's family was cared for by a well-to-do uncle. Hobbes was trained in the elementary subjects, including Greek, in a private school. He was an infant prodigy, who could read and write and do arithmetical calculation at four. He began the study of Latin at six and at fourteen had translated Euripides into Latin. He was educated at Magdalen Hall, Oxford, in the scholastic doctrines then current and seems to have been little impressed by all of it. At graduation he became the tutor or companion of a son of the Earl of Cavendish, a boy only two years younger than himself. He continued as companion and tutor for eighteen years, until the death of his friend, pupil and benefactor, who had been head of his house for two years, with the title of Duke of Devonshire. Then for two years (1629–1631) Hobbes was tutor of a son of Sir Gervase Clifton, but was re-

called by the widow of the Duke of Devonshire as tutor
of her second son and remained a retainer of that family for the duration of his life.

As tutor Hobbes made three journeys in Europe and
became acquainted with most of the great scientists and
literary men, including Galileo. He met Mersenne, a
friend of Descartes, who showed him an early copy of
the *Discours de la Méthode,* but Hobbes was little impressed. He was also acquainted with Bacon, but had
small regard for Bacon's inductive method, although
he respected his learning. Hobbes is said to have been
first impressed with any scholarly work by happening
upon a copy of Euclid, which he read, and which he
used as a model of method in much of his writing. His
psychological and philosophical interest was aroused
when some one asked him what was meant by sense.
This incited him to develop a theory, which was cir-
culated in manuscript, under the title of the *Elements of
Law.* Hobbes always planned to write a comprehensive
treatise in three parts. The first was to discuss the nature of the physical bodies, the second was to treat man,
and the third, the state. He published the last part first in
an abbreviated form as *de Cive,* and later a preliminary sketch of the whole in the *Leviathan,* in English
and Latin. This is the work by which he is best known.
While he worked for twenty years or more upon what
was to be the final form, it was never completed.

Hobbes' life was filled in its middle years by political concern. When the long Parliament impeached Stafford, Hobbes feared that, as the author of the *de Cive* which argued for a strong royalty, he would be in danger, and fled to Paris. In France he became tutor to the Prince of Wales, later Charles the Second, a connection from which he profited after the restoration. After some ten years in France, Hobbes, fearing that the anti-papal attitude he had taken in the *Leviathan* might bring him into conflict with the Church, returned to England in 1651 and there spent the remainder of his days. The latter part of his life was filled with controversy over the religious aspects of his writings. He was frequently accused of atheism, was condemned by the Oxford men for his reflections upon the teaching he had received there in his youth, and quarrelled bitterly with the mathematicians. His life was a stormy one.

Hobbes' empirical attitude towards the problems of psychology has led many to call him the father of empirical psychology, a title that he deserves in many respects. As was said, he became interested in psychology specifically through being asked what was meant by sense. At the time he was interested in mathematics and had been impressed through his meeting with Galileo by the omnipresence of motion. Under this influence he insists that all is motion in the world without and if this be accepted, the mind within must also be explicable by motion. The outside motion acts upon the sense. The sensation is not, however, the mere passive effect of this outside motion. Rather there is always an outwardly directed impulse from within that meets the incoming motion and the sensation arises from the interaction of the two forces. It is the outward moving tendency that leads man to assign the sensation to the object, rather than to regard it as within the mind.

Hobbes spent much time in the analysis of the memory and imagination processes. These are described as mere "decaying sense." No definite distinction is made between memory and imagination. He is more interested in the question why we do not always have awareness of the impression between its origin in sense and its reappearance as memory. He finds the answer by assuming that the fainter elements of "decaying sense" are obscured by the brighter sensations, as the stars are dimmed by the brightness of the sun. They may be detected again when other impressions become faint. Hobbes also recognized the importance of connections between ideas and the original sensations in accounting for their reappearance, what we now know as the laws of association. "Those motions that immediately succeeded one another in the sense continue also together after sense." "Thought is drawn by thought as one bit of water on the table, moved by the finger, draws the rest of the water after it."

He distinguishes two types of trains of thought. One is guided by the intent of the thinker, and the other is unguided and without design. The uncontrolled is illustrated by the frequently quoted instance of the Roman penny. "For in a discussion of our present civil war, what could seem more impertinent than to ask, as one did, 'what was the value of a Roman Penny?' Yet the coherence to me was manifest enough. For the thought of the war introduced the thought of delivering up the king to his enemies; the thought of that brought in the thought of the delivering up of Christ, and that again the thought of the thirty pence, which was the price of that treason: and thence easily followed that malicious question; and all that in a moment of time; for thought is quick." It appears from this that laws of connection can be traced even in thought that is not controlled by a specific intention. Hobbes does not, however, show how specific intention functions, or give its conditions. That problem was not fully appreciated for more than two centuries, and is still not altogether solved.

Hobbes developed his theory of volition or action and feeling or emotion from the same notion of internal movement. He apparently observed that all action is preceded by thought or idea, and then explained it from the principles that had been used in the theory of sensation and imagination. These all depend upon movement within the body and primarily upon movements outward. When these movements are great they produce an actual movement of the members, when they are slight we are aware of them in less degree and then they are known as endeavor. The emotions are derived from the same principle without clear distinction of the differences between emotion and action. These slight movements are also called appetites or desires. These are both positive and negative: when they are towards the object, they are desires, when they are away from them they are aversions. The different types of emotions are compounded of them and differ mainly in degree, in the time of the event, and in the nature of the object. Some reduce to merely verbal problems. Thus desire to know why is curiosity. Deliberation is said to arise from a series of movements, now toward the object, now away from it. Decision is made when the movement turns definitely in one direction.

These motions were rather indefinitely localized. They are in general referred to the heart as in Aristotle, but he nowhere asserts what it is that moves, whether it be animal spirits, or blood, or fluid in general. He is just as indefinite concerning the ultimate nature of the universe without. He asserts specifically that what we call objects are nothing but forms of motion, which are suited to affect us in different ways for each of the qualities of sense, but he does not say what it is that moves, nor does he even speculate about it. All this is characteristic of his empirical spirit. He builds up hypotheses that are sufficient to account for the observed facts, but goes no single step farther than is necessary to understand the phenomena he observes.

It should be said that psychology for Hobbes was merely preliminary to an understanding of the nature of the state and of government. He assumed that men originally dwelt in a condition of mutual warfare and enlightened selfishness alone brought them to agreement with their fellows. Hobbes is interested in man primarily to trace the nature of his impulses and the capacities that made possible this coöperation. While his psychology was the first with an empirical approach and contained many suggestive contributions, he is better known for his political science and general philosophy.

LOCKE

John Locke was more directly influential upon English thought, and upon empirical psychology in general, than Hobbes. For some reason, possibly because he so definitely opposed the church, the universities, and all that the cultivated Englishmen revered, Hobbes was relatively little read in his day and was treated with considerable disdain by those who did read him. He was regarded as an atheist, but did not pique the curiosity of the pious sufficiently to read him. Locke entirely ignores him and writes altogether with reference to Descartes. Thus while Hobbes stands apart from the main line of descent in psychology and philosophy, uninfluenced by Descartes and with little influence upon the men of the next century, Locke is an integral part of the chain, and possibly the man who gave the greatest incentive to the development of the association psychology.

Locke was born at Wrington, a village of Somersetshire, in 1632. His father, an attorney, gave him his early education, which was continued at Westminster School and at Christ Church, Oxford. Like Hobbes, Locke was in later life somewhat disdainful of the teaching at Oxford, although he was successful as shown by his appointment in 1660 to a Greek lectureship. He continued as a scholar at Oxford until political forces led to his dismissal. The connection was more and more formal, as he was frequently away for years at a time, the Scholarship carrying a small annuity and being drawn without reference to services rendered. After graduation, Locke became interested in medicine and studied it irregularly for several years. He never received a medical degree, although he attempted several times to obtain one by special dispensation. He seems to have practised irregularly over a period of years.

He spent two months in 1665 as secretary of an embassy to the Elector of Brandenburg. On his return the following year a chance meeting with Lord Ashley, later Lord Shaftesbury, led to the formation of a lasting connection with that gentleman's family very similar to that of Hobbes with the house of Devonshire. This lasted until 1682. He was in part tutor or general supervisor of their education to two generations of the family, acted as medical adviser, chose a wife for one of the sons, and was counsellor to the head of the house, following his fortunes in good times and in bad. When Shaftesbury was suspected of plotting against the King and fled to Holland in 1682, Locke went with him and continued in exile after Shaftesbury's death until the succession of William of Orange. While in Holland he was introduced into the Court of William of Orange, and after the accession he returned in the company of Mary.

While in the good graces of Lord Shaftesbury, he had some part in drafting the charter for the Carolinas. After the accession of the Oranges, a pamphlet he had written on religious toleration was an important factor in passing the Tolerations Bill, which considerably increased the right to free religious belief. At various times he held minor offices, and had an influence in government circles.

Locke began to write late. His most important work on philosophy and psychology, the *Essay concerning Human Understanding* was published in 1690, when Locke was fifty-eight years old. He had worked on it for ten or a dozen years. Only a few years before he had written his treatise on religious toleration, his first published work of importance. The ten years following the publication of the Essay gave rise to many volumes on a great variety of subjects. During this period Locke lived in semi-retirement at Oates in the home of

Sir Francis Masham. He continued there to his death in 1704.

Locke begins his study of mind with an explicit disavowal of any desire to know what matter is or what is the essence of mind. His object is to study the nature of ideas, by which he means any and all mental contents, then to ask how they give the knowledge that we obtain through them, and in the third place to ask how we determine what knowledge is true. He specifically denies the existence of innate ideas, but insists that all knowledge is derived through the senses, and that the mind at birth is like a clean sheet of paper, a *tabula rasa*, upon which the senses write all that we know. He distinguishes two sources of knowledge, the immediate contributions of sense on the one hand, and reflection, which is a process of working over ideas, on the other. Sensations again are of two sorts, primary and secondary. Primary sensations exist in the object in the same qualities that they induce in us. They are the sensations of size, motion, number, solidity, among others. The secondary sensations, colors, heat and cold, arise in us on the occasion of stimulating the senses, and are not in the object.

Perceptions are made by the combination of sensations. What we call a substance does not exist anywhere as we build it up, but has existence only in our mind. We give it a name and that makes us assume that it has real existence. Exactly how perceptions are built up out of sensations Locke does not say, but that they are compounded out of them he states repeatedly. Reflection mixes with sensation in the development of many perceptions, as when one judges the shape of a sphere from the lights and shades upon its surface. It is in this connection that Locke discusses the problem set by his friend Molyneux, whether a man who had been born blind and through experience had learned to distinguish by touch the difference between a cube and a sphere, could, when he had been given his sight by an operation, be able to distinguish them by sight. Locke answered in the negative and on the whole the answer has been confirmed by the results of actual operations. It also set a problem that has been much discussed ever since in many different phases.

Retention is studied purely empirically without reference to how ideas are retained. Locke asserts that there are two types of memory. In one the material exists merely while it is being considered. In the other, the material vanishes from mind and later returns with the awareness that it has been experienced before. Locke insists that the ideas have no existence when we are not aware of them. Memory is merely the capacity to revive them at will. Ideas are fixed by attention, by repetition, and by the pleasure and pain that are connected with them at the time of the original experience. They are said to fade with time but, if sufficiently often repeated, need never be forgotten. At times the mind is active in recall, behaving as if it were searching for a memory that it needs.

Locke probably stands out most prominently in the history of psychology for formally introducing the term "association of ideas" to explain the process of recall. It is somewhat ironical that Locke made use of the term only incidentally. It did not appear in the first three editions of the *Essay*, and in the fourth was introduced primarily to explain instances of curious departures from ordered thinking. In chapter twenty-three of the second book he points out that if one has eaten too much honey at one time, one takes a dislike to that article of food. Also he mentions an instance of a man who had been cured of a serious disease by a painful operation, and ever after, although extremely grateful to the physician for the cure, could never bear the man's presence because of the pain he had suffered. He explains association as due to the "trains of motion in the animal spirits, which once set going, continue in the same steps they have been used to, which by often treading are worn into a smooth path, and the motion in it becomes easy and, as it were, natural." The explanation is altogether metaphorical, and makes no reference to detailed anatomy. This was characteristic of all of Locke's explanations.

Locke's book had a great vogue almost from the first and continued for a century to be familiar to every educated man. Unlike Hobbes, he was not condemned by the church, although regarded as very advanced in his views. In consequence he had a profound influence upon all later English philosophy. The effect extended to the continent, through the attempted refutation by Leibniz and its adoption by Condillac which was followed in a modified form by many others. Later the empirical spirit embodied in Descartes and in Hobbes was an important factor in determining the attitude of the Encyclopedists and Rousseau. This general spirit and the single fact that it introduced the word "association," giving the explanation it designated new vogue, was Locke's greatest contribution to psychology.

LEIBNIZ

Leibniz has a twofold relation to the history of psychological thought. In the first place, he makes a new attempt to solve the problem of the relation of mind and body that was set by Descartes, and in the attempt hits upon one of the three most important, or at least most generally held, possibilities of picturing that relation. In the second place, he attempts to save deductive thought from the consequences that would logically follow from Locke's conclusions, although they were not drawn by Locke himself. For if all that we know comes from sensation and there are no truths before experience, then one can obtain no truth through reason. We have chosen to treat him in connection with Locke, because of his chronological position mainly, for his spirit is deductive rather than empirical, although his refutation of Locke might give an added justification for the plan.

Leibniz is the first philosophical mind to make its appearance in modern Germany, and might be treated as the founder of German psychology. Born in 1646, the son of a Professor in the University of Leipzig, he early showed great promise. It is said that he studied out Latin by himself, using as a basis the pictures and context in a copy of Livy's history that came into his hands. He was educated in the University of his home city, receiving degrees in mathematics, in law, and finally in jurisprudence. On graduation he was offered a university post but preferred the life of the great world of politics and as a means to that end began the practice of law in Nüremberg. There by chance he became acquainted with a retired statesman, Boinburg by name, who was so impressed by his abilities that he recommended him with success for a small post under the Elector of Mainz. With that beginning he spent the remainder of his life in close dependence upon German noble and royal families. Through these connections he devoted much time to travel; one may especially note his four years' residence in Paris between 1672 and 1676, where he met Malebranche and many other men of distinction. During this period he made two trips to England, had some second-hand correspondence with Newton, and developed his infinitesimal calculus. This last brought him great renown later, but at the time he was accused of having plagiarized Newton. On his return to Germany he had a visit of a month with Spinoza and saw the manuscript of the *Ethics*. He was interested in this primarily to refute it, but it contributed greatly to his philosophical development. Leibniz was attached to the House of Hanover. Officially he was librarian of the Wottelsburg library at Hanover. Later, it is said because he was asked to report on the political events at the court of Frederick the Great for Princess Sophia, he founded the Berlin Academy of Sciences, and was a familiar figure in political and academic circles. He died in Hanover in 1716.

We may emphasize three points in Leibniz's general doctrine that are important for psychology apart from philosophy. These are: first, his theory of the relation of body and mind; second, his introduction of the term apperception; and third, his insistence against Locke that one must have general ideas in the mind itself in advance of experience. Leibniz's picture of the universe essentially determines his attitude towards the first two points. His assumption is that the universe is composed of independent entities that may be represented as thinking atoms. Like the atomists, he refers everything to entities. Unlike the atomists, he assumes that each of these entities is a thinking as well as a material being, and also that they in no way interact upon each other.

Their self-dependence is complete. Every existing thing, from the smallest material particle to God himself, is a *monad*. Each is defined primarily in terms of the degree of consciousness. The material monads have but the vaguest ideas, and from this the range of clearness passes through the animals and man to attain perfect clearness in God. These ideas or conscious processes are representative of events in the universe, but are not induced in the monad by the direct action of any physical force. For this reason he spoke of the monads as "windowless."

This raises the first question to which Leibniz contributed something of importance for psychology, the relation of body and mind. Leibniz's answer to the question, how the presentations of the monads and the events of the outside world might be connected, was that the two were like two perfect clocks which kept the same time without any common control. Both were set going by God at the moment of creation and have gone on at the same rate ever since. In consequence, consciousness in each individual monad mirrors, clearly or vaguely according to its stage of development, the happenings in the world. Leibniz called this the doctrine of preëstablished harmony. When it comes to the relation between body and mind the matter is not so clear although our philosopher worked it out on the same general principle. The body apparently was made up of a vast number of monads each of which had unclear no-

tions only. These kept step with the clear ideas in mind, the dominant monad, as they did with the physical events. Leibniz even provides for a measure of control of body by mind on the assumption that a clear idea might dominate a vaguer one—a perfect monad might set a lead for the imperfect to follow. Leibniz is little concerned with the body in general, and makes no provision for the body to influence the mind. His general notion may be said to be the forerunner of the doctrine of psycho-physical parallelism that was adopted by Wundt, and is still accepted by several authorities. This holds merely that bodily processes and mental processes go on side by side but neither influences the action of the other.

The second in the list of Leibniz's contributions to psychology, his introduction of the term "apperception," developed from grading the ideas in the monads according to their clearness. Just as different monads exhibit different degrees of clearness in ideas, so in the individual human consciousness ideas vary in distinctness. The very faint he calls *petites perceptions* or little perceptions, the very clear are *apperceptions*. Leibniz grants that vague ideas may exist without the monad having awareness of them. Apperceptions are always self-conscious in addition to being clearly conscious. The degree of clearness is also important as a sign of truth. With Descartes, he asserts that what is fully clear is also true, while the vague may be false or uncertain. Then, too, clearness carries with it the tendency to greater strength of action, for ideas are active and the clearer they are the stronger they are. The existence of unconscious ideas and the relation between clearness and activity both continue as elements of the notion of apperception until Wundt, after whose time the term ceased to be generally used.

The third point at which Leibniz affected psychology, although less permanently, was in contending against the sensationalism of Locke. The notion that all knowledge came through the senses was absolutely incompatible with Leibniz's theory. He prepared a work in refutation of the *Essay concerning Human Understanding* paragraph by paragraph. This work was just ready for the press when Locke died, and Leibniz withheld its publication, apparently not to increase the bitterness of the English towards himself, which we have seen was already great because of the charge, now entirely refuted, that he had plagiarized Newton's theory of the calculus. If ideas arise in the monad spontaneously, obviously no knowledge can come through the senses. Leibniz at first insists that no one knows how the senses could be affected or what it would matter if they were. Granted that any knowledge at all comes through the senses it is vague and cannot be relied upon for accuracy. True knowledge is innate. To Locke's axiom that "there is nothing in intellect that was not previously in sense" Leibniz added "except the intellect itself," and

in the most extreme form he made that comprise all
knowledge, at the least, all general and all reliable
knowledge.

In the foregoing chapter, then, we note a process of
return, from the baldly stated sensationalism that approached materialism in Hobbes, through the more
refined and less arbitrary empirical sensationalism of
Locke, back to the most extreme idealism since Plato
in Leibniz. Thus in less than a century of thought man
passed from one extreme to the other. In the next century, thought in Germany and England continues on
its natural course. In Germany, we find the idealistic
tendency confirmed in Kant, after Wolff had reduced
to empty form what he understood of Leibniz. The
English movement, with the addition of radical empiricism, becomes a deistic scepticism in Berkeley, and
gives rise to the extreme scepticism of Hume and the
mechanism of Hartley.

CHAPTER V

ENGLISH EMPIRICISM OF THE EIGHTEENTH
CENTURY: BERKELEY, HUME, AND
HARTLEY

THE trend of English psychology after Locke runs
on towards ever increasing empiricism, although it
shows certain superficial features that seem to imply
a rationalism. The most definitely ambiguous tendency
is shown in Berkeley, who is essentially more empirical
in attitude than Locke, although in one of his theories he
seems to follow an *a priori* line of advance. He starts
with a definitely empirical development and ends in
the conclusion, which would be more in part for Leibniz or Spinoza, that all is God. His final idealism would
seem to be inconsistent with any important contribution
to psychology, yet several of his investigations were
more truly in the spirit of modern psychology than
almost anything that had gone before.

BERKELEY

Berkeley was born in the county of Kilkenny in 1685.
He entered Trinity College, Dublin, in 1700, and after
graduation remained as a fellow until 1713. It was in

88

1709, when only twenty-four, that he published his *New Theory of Vision,* upon which his claim to distinction in psychology really rests. In 1713 he became chaplain to Lord Peterborough, ambassador to Sicily, and was afforded an opportunity in his trips back and forth to become acquainted with men of authority on the Continent. Later he was tutor to the son of the Bishop of Clogher and again lived for two years in France and Italy. In 1722 he formed the project of founding a college in Bermuda for the education of the American Indian, and succeeded in obtaining the passage of a bill in Parliament to supply the funds. While waiting for the actual appropriation of the money he made a trip to Newport, Rhode Island, to investigate the conditions and work out the details of the scheme. The only thing he gained was the forming of a few new acquaintanceships, most important of which was that with Jonathan Edwards. At the end of ten years, Walpole wrote that the money would probably not be forthcoming and Berkeley returned to Ireland. In 1734 he was made Bishop of Cloyne, in the south of Ireland, and lived there until just before his death in 1753. He died at Oxford, where he had gone on his retirement.

As a philosopher, Berkeley is known as the first man specifically to deny the existence of the external world. As a psychologist his most important contribution lay in showing the possibility of an empirical construction of space. Berkeley reached his idealistic position by a very simple extension of Locke's distinction between primary and secondary sensation. Locke said that primary sensations corresponded to actual qualities in the object while secondary sensations existed only in the mind itself. Berkeley asserted that there could be no essential difference between the two. That primary qualities of weight and figure were no more in the object than were colors or sounds. In his later writings, Berkeley asserted that God was the only reality and the justification of the knowledge that apparently came through the senses. God gives two sorts of ideas, those that are intense and vivid, which we ascribe to the external sense, and the less intense, less consistent ideas that we regard as coming from imagination. All have the same source, although the ideas of imagination are but copies of those given directly by the divine spirit.

In his *New Theory of Vision*, Berkeley was interested to learn how we acquire the notion of distance, for distance is a line whose end alone touches the retina and so must be seen as a point. Malebranche and others had suggested that one could estimate the distance of the object both from the angles formed by the rays of light on the retina and from the angles of convergence of the eyes necessary to obtain a single image. Berkeley insisted that we were not at all conscious of either of these angles and so could not use them in estimating distance. Later work has shown that he was correct in the first of these statements and wrong in the second.

He said that actual observation of the individual shows that we are aware of certain changes in the eyes or the images with distance. Near objects are indistinct, but can be made clear by straining the eyes. Distant objects also differ in color from near objects. Berkeley insisted that we do not judge distance as a mathematical problem, but that there is an association formed through frequent connection between the character of the distant object and its distance which makes one call up the other.

Berkeley also used the principle of association to explain the nature of distance. We can actually experience the movement necessary to reach an object, and when a suitable appearance of an object presents itself, it suggests the movement necessary to touch it and this is what we mean by saying that we see distance. He also used this empirical explanation for the interpretation of the size of objects, and to explain why we see objects right side up in spite of the fact that they are inverted upon the retina. All these points are to be explained by the correction of sight by touch, and by the fact that we merely use sight to revive the old tactual experience. He asserts that a man born blind and given his sight by an operation would not see distance, nor correctly interpret the size of objects, nor know whether they were upright or inverted. Only through experience that would enable him to compare sight with touch would these notions develop. It is here that the acuteness of Berkeley in interpreting mental processes shows itself most clearly.

A third point in which Berkeley gives evidence of his empirical bent and also his great keenness in introspection is his insistence that mental processes are always particular. The mental state that represents a general idea is just as particular as the idea of any single object. In fact a general idea itself, Berkeley asserts, is derived from particulars. "An idea which, considered in itself is particular, becomes general by being made to represent or to stand for all other particular ideas of the same sort." This reduction of general to particular and the distinction between the mental state and the object or idea represented did much to eliminate the mystical from English psychology and to make for clear thinking.

Berkeley, then, is a curious instance of a man who, in his philosophy was an idealist and was satisfied by explaining all reality by reference to God, but who in his psychology trusted entirely to observation and would accept nothing as an explanation that could not be verified in his own experience.

HUME

English empiricism culminates in Hume. Locke had eliminated from experience all but the sense impressions and their combinations. He still accepted the existence of objects that were similar to our ideas. Berkeley went a step farther by his denial of the existence of objects at all. He found a justification for the ideas in the fact that God gave and guaranteed them. Only spirit exists as the essence of man and of God who possess the ideas. Hume took the obvious next step by questioning the existence of God and the soul. This left nothing real except sensations and ideas. He thus reached the absolute starting point for all thinking, a premise that took nothing at all for granted.

Hume was born in Edinburgh in 1711. He came of the lesser gentry. Although he matriculated in the University of Edinburgh and attended for a time, he did not complete the work for a degree. He was largely self-educated through reading at home. He tried the law and also business, but found he had no taste for either, and soon abandoned the city to return to the small country place of his parents. He went to France at the age of twenty-three and lived at Rheims and La Flèche, where was the Jesuit school in which Descartes had been educated. While abroad he wrote his *Treatise on Human Nature,* published in 1739, which contains the germ of all his philosophy. The book received only a fairly favorable reception, and was less well regarded in England than abroad. Discouraged by his lack of popular appeal he abandoned philosophy for a time and turned to his *History of England,* which was more successful. After some years he returned to the task of making clear his original thesis in the *Inquiry into Human Understanding*. The two works are alike in the essentials of theory, the second is merely more clearly expressed.

Like most English psychologists, Hume never had a university appointment. In 1744, his friends urged his appointment to a chair of philosophy at the University of Edinburgh, but his doctrines were too much at variance with the belief of the church to make him acceptable. Aside from two minor posts in the foreign service, one on the staff of a mission to Turin, and one as secretary to the ambassador to France, Hume spent the earlier part of his life on the family estate at Ninewells or in Edinburgh. Late in life he was appointed librarian of the Faculty of Advocates in Edinburgh. Like Hobbes he was known as an atheist, and was anathema to the pious. The street on which he lived in Edinburgh was called in derision St. David's Street, and still keeps the name. Hume died in the place of his birth in 1776.

Hume begins with a study of the mental contents that he calls perceptions. Of these, two sorts may be distinguished, impressions that are vivid and strong and ideas which are less clear and fainter. The ideas are exactly like the impressions in the qualities, save only for the difference in strength and vivacity. He is not definite as to the origin of the impressions, although he asserts that there is nothing outside to which they correspond.

In the *Treatise* he speaks as if the appearance of impressions was to be related to motions in the brain and nerves, or movements of the animal spirits, but this is not stated definitely nor elaborated. He specifically refuses to assign any ultimate cause to impressions. They are the given elements from which all else starts but which cannot be explained. Ideas are derived from impressions. He gives a careful description of the processes of memory and imagination, and states that they are to be distinguished by the greater vivacity and clearness of memories, and by the fact that in their order they must repeat the succession in the original impressions. Imagination is free in its reconstruction. Memory and imagination are not faculties but merely names for different ways in which ideas may appear.

Hume also traces the return of impressions in the form of ideas to association. Of associations he distinguishes three forms, resemblance, contiguity in space and time, and cause and effect. Since each impression is distinct from every other, the nature of mental processes is very largely dependent upon association. Hume does not, however, give any explanation of association. In one passage in the *Treatise* he refers to a "path formed by the animal spirits," but does not dwell upon it or seem to take it very seriously. Just as the differences between impressions and ideas are only results of observations, so associations seem to be enumerations of the ways ideas have been seen to follow each other. Hume apparently becomes aware gradually that cause is not on the same level as the other two forms and makes less mention of it in the later work. He even in certain passages, reduces it to a special case of succession.

Out of these simple elements, impressions and ideas, and using only the laws of association, Hume builds up all knowledge. What we call objects are merely different combinations of impressions and ideas. A substance is no more than a firmly associated group of qualities. Similarly there is no self beyond the simple succession of ideas. The fiction that a separate self exists has grown up through a tendency to assume that something exists during the gaps in perception. Thus all is derived from the few simple notions, and nothing is assumed that cannot be observed. The entire series of constructions that are made by the man in the street, as well as the more elaborate concepts of philosophers ancient and modern, were swept away and an attempt made to build anew with the minimum of assumptions. The destructive work had more influence than the constructive, but it should also be said that destruction was more needed than construction. The net result is that Hume's work must be the starting point even now of all philosophy and, on its more theoretical side, of all psychology.

HARTLEY

A contemporary of Hume, but a man who followed his own line of development with little dependence upon Hume, Berkeley or Locke, is Hartley. David Hartley was born at Oxford in 1705, was educated at Cambridge, where he received his A.B. in 1726 and his A.M. in 1729. He was made a fellow the same year but never served, as he forfeited the place by his marriage. Although he had never received the medical degree he began the practice of medicine at Newark and continued it at Bury St. Edmund, London, and at Bath, where he lived until his death in 1757. His psychology is contained in his *Observations on Man*, published in 1749. This work attracted little notice in England until the next century although it was translated into German and had a considerable vogue on the continent. In 1775, Priestley, the chemist and discoverer of oxygen, became interested in the work and had a new edition published, but a quarter century was still to elapse before it had any real appreciation.

Hartley takes the point of view of Hobbes rather more than that of Locke. He was impressed by Newton as Hobbes had been impressed by Galileo. From Newton he learned that all physical things were but forms of motion and he carried the same interpretation over into the mental world. Color is a vibration in the ether, excited by the colored object and extending to the eye. In the eye the vibration is changed from an ether wave to a backward and forward vibration of the nerve and this vibration in the nerve extends to the brain. The brain is to be considered the seat of intelligence. Hartley used Newton's observation of visual after-images to prove that sensory processes once started continue for a time, and explained it as due to the persistence of the vibrations when once started. He applied the same idea to explain all memory. When the substance of the brain has once been set into vibrations, the oscillations continue with diminishing strength. These slight vibrations he called *vibratiuncles,* and asserted that all memories were due to them. The arousal of the slight vibrations was by means of association. When two sensations affect the nervous system at the same time or in succession, they become connected in such a way that whenever one is later reëxcited the vibrations extend from it to the other and we have an idea of that other. The ideas are always fainter than the original sensations. Hartley also noted that in association between successive impressions, the first always arouses the second, but the second will not arouse the first. He deserves credit for noticing that ideas of smell, touch and taste are fainter and less frequent than are those of sight and hearing. This was one of the first cases in which differences in imagery are mentioned and in so far it anticipates Galton and Charcot.

We thus see that Hartley has a definitely materialistic

interpretation of mental phenomena, in which for the first time the animal spirits are entirely superseded. He is at pains to insist that the nerves are solid and not tubes as had always been asserted before him, so that nothing could flow through them, while it makes vibrations pass through them much more readily. Hartley extended his theory to cover all mental operations. Movements arise when the vibrations active in sensation pass over into the muscle and excite other vibrations there which produce the contractions in the muscle. This is a very definite anticipation of the law of ideo-motor action—that is, that all movement is determined by or grows out of idea or sensation.

Many specific problems were recognized and attempts made to solve them by the principles of vibration and association. Pleasure was designated as the result of a vibration kept well within due limits, while pains are vibrations so intense as to surpass those limits. What determines those limits Hartley does not attempt to state. After he makes this statement of the conditions of pleasure and pain, he develops through the principle of association the various extensions of the notions that constitute the simpler emotions. All emotions are compounded of sensations and of the simple pleasures and pains. The classification shows how a pleasure may be extended from the original situation to new ones, and thus secondary affections arise. Emotions also influence actions, as pleasures lead to desire and so to approach, while pains give rise to aversions and so to withdrawal. Hartley also has a discussion of the nature of language based on the general laws of association that was much used by later writers.

On the whole, Hartley may be said to have made the first serious attempt to develop a physiological psychology. His principles were more nearly adequate than any of his predecessors in this field, and he made a consistent application of them over a wider range. At the same time he elaborated the fullest explanation of the mental life in terms of association up to the end of his century. James Mill followed closely in his footsteps in this phase of the work, although Mill made no use of the physiological hypotheses. It was not until the beginning of the nineteenth century that Hartley had any great appreciation. It is interesting to note that while Hartley is generally looked upon as a materialist and as atheistical in his teachings, he did not have this intention in the least. He apparently regarded his theory as bearing only upon the bodily mechanism and would have the mind standing above and in some definite relation to the body. He does not, however, make clear what this relation is. In the third part of his work, which is usually not read, he developed a theory of religion from the orthodox standpoint. Priestley did not republish this part and emphasized the materialistic aspects of the theory. Hartley would probably have been greatly sur-

prised were he to become aware of the anti-religious interpretation that was put upon his work as a whole.

CONDILLAC

An important reverberation of the work of Locke and the English empirical attitude in general was seen on the continent, especially in the work of Etienne de Condillac. Condillac was born in 1715 on the small estate of his family at Flux, near Beaugency in the Dauphiné. He lived there quietly all his life save for the ten year period from 1758–1768, which he spent at Parma as the tutor of the son of the Duke, who became Duke Ferdinand and was the uncle of Louis XV. He was at one time intimate with Rousseau and with several of the Encyclopedists but did not long continue the connection. He also showed his retiring disposition by taking little part in the sittings of the Academy although he was for a long time a member.

In his first book, a *Treatise on the Origins of Human Knowledge*, 1746, he did little more than reproduce Locke's theories. More original and of much greater influence was his *Treatise on Sensations* (*Traité des sensations*), published in 1754. In this work he asked himself what would happen if a human soul were imprisoned in a marble statue, at first without any means of receiving impressions from the outside, and then should begin to develop sense organs. The mind was assumed to be without traces of knowledge, although with the usual capacities for development. He chose smell as the first sense to unfold, because it is the simplest, and attempted to show what would happen as various sensations were received. The first sensation to appear must necessarily prepare the way for all similar ones and thus he explains attention. In part attention must be due to the natural predispositions of the mind to receive one quality rather than another, in part it is determined by the sensations that have already been received. He defines attention as the mere vividness of the sensations themselves.

All other faculties are derived from the sensations. When two different sensations are experienced in succession differences and similarities appear, and in this consists comparison, if differences are observed, and judgment, if attention is given to the similarities. Memories are only sensations that return a second time. They are fainter than sensations but otherwise are the same. Pleasure and pain are also immediate aspects of sensations and no sensation lacks one of these characteristics. Movement arises when there is either a painful sensation or the memory of a pleasant sensation at a distance. Movement follows directly upon sensation and the manner of the moving is determined by the pleasure or pain that attaches to the sensation.

After smell has been fully developed, Condillac con-

siders how the addition of other senses affect the man.
When touch develops, the statue might become aware of
the surface of his body through exploring it. With these
exploring movements notions of space would develop.
When the eyes are opened to receive impressions, the
mind is transformed by the new riches of experience.
The sensations from sight are understood in terms of the
experiences earlier developed through the other senses.
Without the ideas of space that are derived from touch,
vision could not give an idea of distance or of other
spatial values. When the motions are derived from
touch, the interpretation of objects as extended is soon
acquired by matching the sensations received from
touch with the simultaneous excitations of the retina.
Thus Condillac derived all the complicated as well as
the simplest mental operations and capacities from
sensation.

The vivid method of presentation and the absolute
simplicity of explanation gave Condillac's statue great
vogue. It impressed the Encyclopedists and supplied
much of their philosophy. Rousseau shows its influence,
and French philosophy for nearly a century went back
to him for many of its inspirations. The break with the
past that opened the way for the French Revolution was
prepared for by notions similar to Condillac's. Condillac may be regarded as a contributing cause to that
universal empiricism, or he may be looked upon as
another evidence of the general loosening of ancient

intellectual traditions, which was transferred to political and social thinking.

BONNET

More directly influenced by Condillac is Bonnet, (1720–1793) the Swiss naturalist. Bonnet is entitled to credit as one of the first careful observers of the behaviour of ants and as such he made contributions that were useful to later animal psychology. In his *Essai de Psychologie,* published anonymously in 1754 at Leyden, Bonnet followed Condillac in using the analogy of the statue in tracing the development of mental capacities. He acknowledges his indebtedness with the statement that he had thought of assuming that his statue had developed sight first, as the most important and most used sense, but after reading Condillac had followed his example in giving smell precedence. Bonnet differs from Condillac in that he gave his statue a nervous system as well as a mind, and he follows Hartley rather closely in the physiological explanation of the mental life. He says that the scent of the rose when first presented to the statue causes, by the vibrations that constitute it, a series of oscillations in the sense organ and sensory nerves. These are propagated to the brain and there cause the conscious processes. The notion is expanded along principles very similar to Hartley's. Unlike Hartley, however, he specifically assumes a mind in addition to the vibrating nervous system and regards the two as running parallel. He both combined and developed the systems of Hartley and Condillac.

CHAPTER VI

GERMAN PSYCHOLOGY IN THE EIGHTEENTH CENTURY: WOLFF, KANT, AND TETENS

THE development of a strictly national psychology, possibly the development of a national scholarly discipline in general, was rather slower in Germany than in the neighboring states. In spite of the early signs of a break with the older religious teachings, as evidenced by the work of Luther, Melancthon, and others, German education held to the scholastic forms until well into the eighteenth century. This is seen partly in the slow development of the use of German in scholarly books. While Descartes and Hobbes in the seventeenth century were writing by preference in French and English respectively, although they did have their works translated into Latin or written in Latin also for scholars of other lands, we find Leibniz a generation later writing in Latin or, when he departed from it, in French, rather than in his native tongue.

This is partly due, no doubt, to the fact, that aside from Leibniz, German scholars were almost all connected with the universities, while French and English psychologists and philosophers were outside of the

scholastic atmosphere. Each of the men we have discussed as making a contribution to the history of psychology was by profession a soldier, a statesman, or a
private tutor. Locke and Hobbes complain bitterly of
the futile scholasticism of the English universities of
the period, as still strongly dominated by the monastic
tradition. Before the nineteenth century we find no
Briton of distinction in psychology connected with a
university, and aside from the Scotch School, the same
held for the first part of the nineteenth century as well.
In Germany, on the contrary, from Leibniz on, every
German psychologist of distinction was a professor in
a university and so subject more fully to the academic
tradition. German universities were no more backward
than those elsewhere, but psychology elsewhere was
written by independent scholars, and in Germany, when
written at all, was the work of the university men.

A brief word may be said of the organization and
especially of the grades of the German universities of
the eighteenth century, an organization that holds until
the present. In general they were state supported, and
controlled directly by the minister of education. They
were all looked upon as assemblages of scholars who
should be free to do as they pleased in all their scholarly work, but appointments were made by the central
minister of education. A man was first appointed as a
privat docent, who received nothing more than permis-
sion to teach and had no stipend save a portion of the

fees paid by students who attended his lectures. As openings came by the death or resignation of his seniors he was advanced to the rank of *ausserordentlicher Professor,* a title which carried a small salary, and then to the full title of *ordentlicher Professor*. Except in extraordinary circumstances appointments to the higher ranks were for life.

WOLFF

The first of the academic psychologists we have to notice was Wolff. Leibniz as we have seen was connected with the court, and his nearest approach to an academic post was his secretaryship of the Berlin Academy. Wolff, who followed him in time and was in many respects his disciple, was a typical university professor in his career and some would say even in his pedantry. He was born at Breslau in 1679. He received his Ph.D. degree from Jena and later was professor at Halle. The one event that broke the even tenor of his academic life occurred in 1723 when the orthodox citizens secured his dismissal from the university because they regarded his teachings as atheistical. He found a refuge in the chair of philosophy at Marburg. He finally triumphed over his accusers and in 1740 was reinstated at Halle by Frederick the Great with great ceremony.

Wolff wrote scholarly works in Latin and numerous text-books in German. He apparently was among the first to teach in German, and had a considerable influence in promoting the use of the vernacular in the universities, as his texts went through numerous editions because of their wide use. His two Latin works, *Psychologia empirica* (1734) and *Psychologia rationalis* (1754) contain the extended statement. It is said that this was the first time that the word psychology was used in the title of a book, although Melancthon had applied the word to describe the subject matter. Wolff is frequently stated to have organized Leibniz's scattered statements about psychology and put them into teachable form, but he did much more than that. He was definitely influenced by Leibniz, but he transformed almost every feature of his system, so that at the end there is little in it that is not more his own than his predecessor's.

Wolff makes mind very much more a real force, and also assigns a much more important function to the body. Instead of merely mirroring events, because of the orderly unwinding of its own nature, mind is a real, active force and ideas are also active agents. The only remnant of preëstablished harmony is the statement of a psycho-physical parallelism in much its modern form. That is, the ideas run their course at the same rate as the corresponding bodily process, but neither is to be regarded as the determinant of the other. He neglects to say how they are kept together. The body process is much more specific than in Leibniz. Wolff even speaks of material ideas, which he does not however more closely describe, that are the accompaniments of the mental processes.

A second indication of the greater importance and independence of mind is seen in the place Wolff gives to the notion of faculties, which he developed to a striking degree. Mind is divided first into the faculties of knowing and of feeling or desire. The faculty of knowing is again divided into several others. It involves first the faculty of perception or sensing. This is completed and perfected by the faculty of imagination. Memory is the faculty of retaining and has several forms. Understanding is the faculty of clearly ideating that which is possible, and so of distinguishing, judging and forming general concepts. Pure reason is the power of drawing conclusions from pure concepts. Feelings are divided into pleasure and pain. Usually he speaks as if the feelings were independent of knowledge, but at times he makes pleasure correspond to the appreciation of adequacy, and pain to inadequacy. Will follows directly from feeling and, as with Aristotle, they were put in the one class of appetition.

These faculties did not prevent a considerable amount of clear, detailed analysis. Thus attention was made the capacity for clearing up ideas, and it was asserted that the extent of the field of attention varied with the degree of clearness, a wide field implying less clearness than a restricted field. One is said to control the course of recall by attending to ideas that are similar to, or that have on another occasion accompanied or preceded, the idea that one desires to recall. The will is made a free agent in general, thus opposing Leibniz who gave God alone freedom in choosing one from among the many possible worlds. After that all was determined. Wolff also continued the use of Leibniz's term "apperception" to designate the clearness of ideas, and tended to connect it with attention.

Wolff's psychology supplanted the Aristotelian teachings in the universities of Germany, and his text-books had a great influence in spreading the use of the German language, at once a sign and a cause of the wane of scholasticism. It was in the psychology of Wolff that Kant developed, and the influence of his system was strong on all the later Germans.

KANT

Immanuel Kant (1724–1804) probably, next to Aristotle, had the greatest influence upon philosophical thought of any man, and has a claim to be the greatest philosopher of all time. As a philosopher he may be said to have recognized the ideals of the continental and English schools and to have compromised their differences in a new attitude. He saw the impossibility of discovering the fundamental entities that were demanded by the continentals, but he did not accept the complete denial of all that lay beyond immediate experience which Hume had attempted to make. He replaced both by saying we must give a critical analysis of the possibilities of knowledge. He initiated a method that dominated the next generation, and which still has a very great influence on all philosophy. His ideals were not in harmony with psychological work, so that he advanced it little and may even be said to have delayed its coming into prominence.

Kant had the same quite uneventful academic life as Wolff. Born in the small university town of Königsberg, near the extreme eastern frontier of Prussia, he never went more than a few miles from it in his whole life. He was of Scotch ancestry. He studied at the University of his birthplace and after receiving his doctorate was for several years a tutor in country families nearby. In 1755, his writings had attracted sufficient notice to lead to his appointment as *docent* in the University; he was made *ordentlicher* Professor in 1770, and continued a regular routine of teaching and writing until his death in 1804. No life could be outwardly less exciting or even less interesting.

In his early writings Kant did little more than elaborate and criticize Wolff's doctrines. He showed great learning and acuteness but gave no signs of a break with his immediate past. He himself says that reading Hume woke him from his dogmatic slumber and forced him to face a problem hitherto not appreciated. Hume asserted that we could know only sensations and ideas that were derived from sensations, that the physical object on the one side, and the soul as a substance on the other, were not found in experience. Kant admitted that Hume's criticism of the naive assumptions of earlier psychology was just, but he was not willing to accept Hume's conclusion that all rational knowledge was impossible. On the contrary, he was so convinced of the truth of that knowledge and of the necessity for accepting it that he made its existence the primary assumption, and asserted that no theory of mind and nature which did not permit of that truth could hold. On the contrary, any construction that would make possible a belief in the efficacy of knowledge must be true. Kant therefore sought to build up a theory of knowing that would permit certain deductions which might hold under all circumstances.

We are saved from a detailed treatment of his theory by the fact that it is epistemology rather than psychology, but may outline one or two points which have a bearing upon psychology and have determined some of its theories. Kant admitted that the soul itself is never known, and the object outside is never known directly, although he believes that some unknown force exists both within and without. The thing-in-itself, the unknown force without, supplies the raw material; the transcendental self within supplies the capacity for organization. The organizing forces within are arranged in ascending importance. First the raw material is given extent and duration by being taken into the forms of space and time. Since these forms are in the mind and are applied to objects of all sorts, one can know them in advance, and so can make the rational deductions of geometry and mechanics. This was important for later psychological theory as it led to the belief on the part of one school that space was innate, and was, at the most, only developed by experience. Kant also assumed that important relations which exist between sensation, such as cause and effect, were innate and were added to the sensations in the process of understanding them.

In 1798, that is, much after his other more philosophical works, Kant wrote a brief treatise on psychology which he called *Anthropology in its Practical Aspects*. It is a popular and, even for that day, somewhat superficial sketch of mental processes. He is interested in the explanation of why we remember and forget certain things, in the different types of imagination, in the explanation of prevision, divination, and dreams. He took a sceptical attitude towards divination and previsions, from the fact that these were not in harmony with a freedom of the individual will. The other topics were treated in essay fashion, and the facts were drawn from common observation and tradition.

The treatise was divided into three parts, the first on the faculty of knowledge, the second on feelings, and the third on appetition. The first treated the sensations,

imagination, and memory, sagacity, wit, and originality or genius. The second was a discussion of pleasure
and pain in their different aspects. The third began with
the faculty of desire and passed over to emotions in general and from that to temperament and character, with
the differences exhibited by the different races and
sexes. On the whole it is the type of essay that any wide-
awake man of broad learning but no special study of psychology might have written. How general were the
sources from which the material is drawn is seen from
the fact that almost the only authority quoted is Field-
ing, the novelist. Kant does not seem to have intended
it to be, and it certainly is not, a serious contribution to
psychology.

Kant's influence upon psychology may be summed
up in three positive and two negative contributions. Of
his theories favoring the development of psychology,
there was first the banishment of the mind or soul as
an immediate object of study, which tended ultimately—
though it must be confessed this influence was considerably delayed—to favor the empirical study of mental
processes and human actions rather than speculation
about the nature of the soul. Secondly, there was the
development of the notion that space was subjective
and an innate property of mind. This developed into the
nativistic theories that have been advocated and dis-
puted by different schools down to the present. Thirdly,
there was the establishing of the threefold division of

mental processes, into intellect, feeling, and will, as opposed to the twofold classification into intellect and appetition that had persisted from the Greeks. It must be said that this third contribution was indirect, if not unintentional, on Kant's part. What led to it was apparently the writing of three critiques. The *Critique of Pure Reason* treated the intellectual process. The *Critique of Judgment* dealt with pleasures, especially with aesthetic enjoyment, and the *Critique of Practical Judgment* dealt with action, especially with the ethical features of action. Kant's followers later carried over the division of the three books to justify three distinct functions. As a matter of fact, in the *Anthropologie*, Kant does not distinguish between emotion and action, while the third book discusses merely the emotional processes, and says no more of action or volition than does Aristotle under the head of appetition. It seems rather that the frequent mention of the three critiques gradually suggested the division of the mental life into three corresponding parts, and when this division was accepted it was ascribed to Kant.

Kant delayed the development of psychology indirectly by turning attention from the empirical study of mental processes and human behavior to argument over what it was necessary to assume if man should be capable of attaining truth through reasoning. This rationalizing type of investigation dominated Kant's immediate successors on the philosophical side, Fichte,

Schelling, and Hegel, to the extent that they lost all interest in observation or experiment with either mental or physical phenomena. Psychology had no chance in Germany until this tendency ran itself out, which required nearly a generation. In the second place, Kant set up as a criterion for a science that it deal only in exact measurements and that mathematics may be applied to it. Mental states, he asserted, could not be measured, and so could not be brought into the field of mathematics. Kant was led to this point of view because he knew only physics and chemistry. Biology was just beginning to develop and could hardly be called a science. Psychology did not fall into the pattern set by physics and so could not be a science. This dogma of Kant did more to delay the development of psychology than anything he did in its favor. It also started several of the men who sought to develop a science of mind on the wrong scent. They endeavored to measure in ways that were futile and set up the forms of mathematics where the substance was lacking. On the whole, Kant delayed rather than furthered the progress of psychology.

TETENS

A contemporary of Kant and one who, had he not been overshadowed by Kant, would have had a large place in philosophy and psychology, was Nicolai Tetens (1736–1807). He was a man well acquainted with the works of the English and French as well as the Germans, and at the same time keen in direct observation and in criticism of the works of others. In spite of his brilliancy, he was almost lost to sight by the generation that followed him and only appreciated nearly a century later. Tetens was born in Schleswig in 1736 or 1738, the record being uncertain. He studied in the universities of Rostock and Copenhagen and was *docent* in the University of Rostock in 1759. He continued there until the Prussian conquest of Mecklenburg forced the transfer of the university to Bützow. In 1776 he was called to the University of Kiel and soon after to Copenhagen as professor. In 1789 he was asked to assume an important post in the finance ministry of Denmark and gradually advanced until he became head of the finances of the state. He continued to give most of his time to administration until his death in 1807.

Tetens wrote on numerous subjects, but his reputation in psychology rests upon his *Versuche über die menschliche Natur* (*Essay on Human Nature*), published in 1777. It is a thoroughly empirical study of mental processes and at many points anticipates the discoveries of the next century. It is a mixture of the tendencies of the English empiricists and the French sensationalists with the more rationalistic continental trend. Following Locke and Hume, he begins his discussion with a study of the relations between sensations and ideas. He asserts that ideas are due to the later rearousal of the traces left by sensations. He anticipates Fechner in his statement that memories are related to sensations as the visual after-images to the original stimulation. The one remains in the brain as the other in the eye. The preface discusses at length the vibration theory of Hartley and its modifications by Bonnet. He objects to regarding vibrations as the cause of memories, for he rightly believes that it would be very difficult for any vibration to persist as long as memories do. He would substitute for vibrations a slower movement of greater duration, and points out that the brain is made of some peculiar substance that would make such movements possible. He grants quite frankly that this is merely an hypothesis and makes no attempt to conjecture what the nature of the substance might be.

He makes introspection, which he calls the "inner sense," the primary method of studying mental processes. He foresees the objection later made explicit by Comte, that introspection involves a double observation, observation of the state itself and again observation of the process of observation. Tetens also saw the remedy, now nearly universally recognized, for this difficulty; namely, that one can, and in fact always does, study not the state itself, but the primary memory of it which retains all the characters of the original. The observing does not then interfere at all with the course of the original mental state.

Tetens is an associationist and accepts contiguity in

space and time and similarity from Hume's lists of the forms of association. Hume's reduction of cause and effect to mere frequent succession of two events he cannot believe. He remarks that many events succeed each other frequently and never come to be regarded as one the cause of the other unless something peculiarly favors that interpretation. He is at some difficulty to determine what the factor is that is necessary to make possible the causal interpretation and finally decides that the answer can be found in the harmony of this special case with the established laws of thought.

Many other points are made that have a very modern flavor. He distinguishes between the idea itself and the meaning that attaches to it. He holds that one may think with perfect clearness when the images that carry the meaning are vague, and that one may be confused in thought when the separate ideas are clear enough. He has a theory that the feeling of truth or belief arises from a harmony between the particular conclusions and the sum of knowledge that the thinker possesses, or so much of it as is active at the moment. He recognizes the fact of attention in the statement that perception involves not merely the reception of the impressions, but also an antecedent preparation by applying different activities of the mind to prepare the way for them.

Feeling and emotion are treated, but in a subordinate way. In the question of action, he is most interested in considering whether man is free. He does indicate that all action grows out of sensation and is directed by sensation and idea. The first time an act is performed, however, it is an instinctive expression of the nature of the mind. It arises immediately and freely. When it is repeated it grows out of an idea of the earlier occasion and a memory of the feelings that resulted from and accompanied it. Tetens traces the degrees of clearness of the ideas and sensations that will lead to the production of an actual movement. He points out that one can think of an act in a vague way and have no act result; increase the definiteness of thought, of a word, for example, and the lips move but no sound results; recall the exact movement, and speech follows. The idea of the act in this case stands to the actual act much as the real sensation stands to the memory of it.

On the whole Tetens' work is an admirable combination of clear-seeing criticism and originality. He keeps all the best of the English school that rejects all arbitrary assumption of mystic forces and faculties, and at the same time he is aware that in many instances this school overlooked real problems. He always appealed to direct observation when in doubt and enriched his contribution in many points by its results. Psychology lost greatly by the failure of others to appreciate the results and pursue the methods of Tetens. In spirit he was a century ahead of his time. It is interesting to speculate on what the result would have been had Tetens instead of Kant become the acknowledged leader of the thought of the early nineteenth century. The problem is complicated by the fact that Tetens had gone about as far as was possible without a great advance in the other empirical sciences. Perhaps this in part accounts for the slight influence he had upon the history of thought.

CHAPTER VII

THE SCOTCH AND BEGINNINGS OF THE MODERN ENGLISH SCHOOLS

WHILE Germany was passing from the formalism of Wolff to the advanced criticism of Kant that resulted in the temporary occlusion of psychology within her borders, England was attempting to deal with Hume's scepticism in a less radical way. The Englishman rather crudely denied Hume's attack on knowledge and did not attempt to resolve it.

REID

The men who developed the first method of replying to Hume's argument are known as the Scottish school since they were all professors in the Scotch Universities. The first of the group was Thomas Reid, born at Strachan, Scotland, in 1710, and Professor of Philosophy at St. Andrews from 1752 to 1763 and at Glasgow from 1763 until his death in 1792. Reid argued against Hume that we must believe in the external world or our mental states would be a delusion, and that we actually know mind immediately and directly. Like all the Scotch school, he had nothing to say of the body or brain, and treated mental states as independent and separate. Belief in the outside world was guaranteed by what he called "common sense," always a vague term, which seems to come down to the statement that it would be foolish not to believe.

Reid's psychology was largely associationism after the manner of Locke, although he specifically repudiates the term. Ideas, he says, are recalled through the "inductive principle," but in practice this designation amounted to exactly what is meant when it is said they are recalled by association. In other respects his psychology was of the simple faculty type. The mind had a special power or capacity for each of the functions that are given a name in ordinary usage. These are treated entirely uncritically. The will is a free faculty, that may take motives into account but is not determined by them. Reid had some influence as a philosopher, but did little for or against psychology.

STEWART

Dugald Stewart, who was next in the Scotch succession, was born at Edinburgh in 1753, and was Professor of Philosophy in the University there at the time of his death. Rather a rhetorician and orator than a scholar, he contributed least of all the members of the school to either philosophy or psychology. In the main a follower of Reid, he may be mentioned only for giving a place to attention as directing recall and in filling the gaps that may be left in the association series.

THOMAS BROWN

Thomas Brown, born at Kirkmabreck in 1778, was the most original of the group. He was educated at Edinburgh, trying law and medicine in turn, and philosophy as a life work only after a period of practice in the latter. He was a versatile individual as shown by the fact that in addition to his work in law and medicine, he spent quite as much time writing verse as philosophy, though his verse was never taken seriously by others. He occupied the chair of philosophy in succession to Stewart from 1810 until his death in 1820. Brown came under the influence of Condillac and Destutt de Tracy as well as that of Stewart. He also knew Kant's work, but judging by a review he wrote in the Edinburgh Review early in life, did not understand him thoroughly.

Brown showed the influence of his medical training by giving what is for that day a very thorough treatment of sensation. The most original contribution came in his recognition of the muscle sense, and in showing what it must add to the skin senses in the interpretation of objects. Sir Charles Bell had already recognized the presence of sensory as well as motor nerves in the muscle, which may have served as a suggestion to Brown.

Like all of his school he was very loath to recognize the association processes as important, although like them too, he brings in the fact under another name. He calls the process "suggestion," and finds three laws of suggestion—contiguity in space and time, resemblance and contrast. He intimates that a more refined analysis would probably reduce all to some form of contiguity. He again divides the laws of suggestion into two more general classes: a simple suggestion, which he would use to explain memory, imagination and the connections of feeling and emotional states, as well; and relative suggestion, which he would employ in the more complicated processes of judgment, comparison, abstraction, and generalization.

Brown gives a very keen description of reasoning as a natural product of the laws of suggestion. He asserts that thought is not subject to voluntary control, but follows purely chance orders, dependent upon the conditions of the moment and the experience of the individual. He opposes these to the laws of formal logic, which do not correspond to the actually observed order of thinking. Many observations in this part show great keenness and anticipate recent discussions. He devotes a large part of his published lectures to the discussion of emotion, but this degenerates into sermonizing, with no value for psychology. Exception might be made of occasional passages that point out the control of emotion by the laws of resemblance.

The Scotch school as a whole constitutes a strange interlude in the progress of psychology. It was an attempt to save the conventional treatment of the subject from the attacks, as they thought them, of Hume, and even more of Hartley. It was largely motivated by the orthodox demands of the Scotch church, and it judged conclusions more from the bearing they might have on the accepted dogmas of the church than from their inherent truth. The contributions of its members to psychology were made almost in spite of their principles, and are very few.

HAMILTON

A Scotchman who stands on the border line of the Scotch school is Sir William Hamilton, better known for his work in logic than in psychology. He was born in Glasgow in 1788, was educated at the universities of Glasgow and Oxford, and began active life as an advocate. In 1821 he was made Professor of History at Edinburgh, and transferred to the chair of Logic and Metaphysics in 1836. He died in 1856. Hamilton is known as the greatest scholar of the Scotch school. He knew his Kant well and had read widely in continental philosophy, and also was personally acquainted with many of the philosophers through his travels. He was thoroughly educated in the classics and knew and appreciated Aristotle. He wrote no work that claims to be specifically psychology, but did make contributions to psychological problems.

Hamilton's philosophy and psychology embodied almost all the tendencies of his earlier compatriots. He, too, was interested in establishing the existence of external objects, which he did by the same reference to common sense. He saw the relations between the Scotch theory of mental processes and a world without which must be accepted by common sense but is not directly known, and Kant's interpretation which distinguished the actual phenomenon of consciousness from the thing-in-itself.

Hamilton's psychology was of the faculty type. He believed in an active mind that controlled mental states, while mind as a whole directed the actions of the individual. His specific faculties all dealt with the cognitive or knowing states. He enumerates six of these: the faculty of perception, which directs the entrance of knowledge; the faculty of preservation, which retains ideas; the reproductive faculty, which brings them again into consciousness; the representative faculty, which holds them clearly before mind; the elaborative faculty, which compares and relates different ideas and sensations and thus develops concepts; and finally the "over-faculty," which controls all and is especially active in developing *a priori* reasoning. This last faculty also is the source of belief, which Hamilton, from religious considerations, regarded as being capable of accepting conclusions that were not justified by knowledge. Apparently, the religious man must believe whether the tenet of faith is or is not in accordance with his experience.

Hamilton's most important contribution to empirical psychology was his doctrine of redintegration. To all the Scotch school, the picture of mind as composed of distinct elementary ideas that are derived from sensation by revival as a result of the connections formed at the time of an earlier experience, was highly distasteful. It did not give enough play to the active mind and its subordinate faculties. Each of the Scotchmen, as we have seen so far, gave up the name, although he continued to recognize the fact in another guise. None could escape the observation that the order of return of ideas followed the order of the original sensations. Hamilton was no exception to the rule. For him the striking characteristic was that one part of an experience always tended to recall the whole. He called this redintegration. This gave at least a suggestion of activity to mind. Possibly it may have grown out of seeing that elements recalled different ideas when in one whole from those recalled in another. The phenomenon had been described earlier in this way by other men, but Hamilton hit upon it independently and gave it a temporary vogue. The return of the Mills to Hartley's conception of association obscured it for a generation, but it was revived by Bradley, the logician, and still more recently by Hollingworth.

The faculty psychology of the Scotch school made a break in the true empirical tradition of the British school. The English school throughout had depended upon direct observation with a minimum of interest in explanation by means of fundamental existences that were developed as hypotheses. The lapse was not for long. We may regard Hume as the last of the earlier English school. Contemporaneously with Hamilton, the modern English school began to develop.

JAMES MILL

Modern English psychology may be said to have begun with the work of James Mill. James Mill, the son of a rural shoemaker, was born at Northwater Bridge, Forfarshire, in 1773. Through the friendship of a nobleman, he was educated at Edinburgh for the ministry. He was not much interested and not successful in that calling and moved to London where he supported himself by literary work. His first book of importance was a *History of India,* which won for him not only recognition, but a place in the East India Company which he held for life. In London he early came under the influence of Bentham and was soon one of the leaders in the Utilitarian movement. Through this he acquired considerable political influence. Mill's important psychological work was the *Analysis of the Human Mind*, which he began about 1820 and completed in 1829.

In psychology, Mill was most influenced by Hartley, although at Edinburgh he had been a student of Stewart whose eloquence he admired. Mill's theory developed strictly on the basis of association. Unlike Hartley he makes no use of anatomy, but considers only the mental processes. His work begins with a list of the sensations that provide the material of knowledge. Here again there is no more than mention of the sense organ. No attempt is made to describe it or its mechanism, or to relate the action of the organ to the sensation. The usual five senses are described briefly, and to them are added the sense of muscular contraction and senses from the alimentary canal. Muscular contraction is made much of in the interpretation of the more complex mental phenomena, as space and time. In this he follows Hartley and Brown.

A discussion of ideas follows upon the sensations. Here Hume's mark can be seen in Mill's doctrine that ideas are the remnants of the sensations. The remnants are rearoused through association. Mill reduced the forms of association to contiguity in space and time, to the synchronous and the successive. Hume's causation was said to be mere succession, his similarity being due to the fact that similar objects had frequently been presented together, and his law of contrast arising from the simultaneous occurrence of the objects that are contrasted. Memory is nothing more than the fact of recall through association. The reappearance of a sensation, together with the fact that we associate with it the time when and the place where it has previously been presented, is all that is involved in memory. Generalization is made possible by the use of language. This again is nothing more than the association of the word with the sensations or groups of sensations in such a way that the word stands for or represents the object or idea. Abstraction arises from connecting the same word with a number of different but similar objects, or qualities. The words developed in this way may be treated as themselves objects in so far as they form associations both with each other and with things just as sensations and ideas do.

The general empirical spirit of Mill can be seen particularly clearly in his treatment of belief. This he sees to be involved in each of the more complicated mental operations. Most writers, he asserts, incline to make something of a mystery of the process. He insists, however, that it can be reduced to the simple elementary processes. Sensations if intense or clear arouse belief. Ideas are accepted if the associations that bring them back are strong. Propositions are believed because of the closeness of association between the words that are involved in them and some other word, idea, or sensation.

The same type of explanation is applied to pleasure and pain and to the active or voluntary processes. Pleasure and pain are regarded as immediate sensations, but through association the pleasure and pain become extended to all else that is connected with them, to the antecedent sensations that are accepted as their cause and to objects that were present at the time they were first experienced, whether or not they can be regarded as the cause of the pleasure or of the pain. When the object that is pleasant is merely anticipated, we have desire. This pleasant idea is the antecedent and may be regarded as the cause of movements. Movements of the body follow directly upon sensations and ideas. If the sensation or idea is pleasant, the movement is one of approach; if it is unpleasant, the movement is one of withdrawal. When the idea is of a distant end, the series of movements may be long continued. In that case we are said to act through desire. In no case need we asume any power or force in addition to the idea. Mill had no place for the will as a force apart from the separate sensations and ideas that compose or accompany it. Mind was for him nothing in addition to the sensations, ideas, and feelings that constitute the mental states.

JOHN STUART MILL

James Mill's theory was expounded and his work continued by his son, John Stuart Mill. John Stuart Mill was born in Pentonville, a suburb of London, in 1806. He was educated almost exclusively by his father, who taught him Greek with his English and in general pushed him into advanced subjects much earlier than the schools would attempt to do. While still very young he was given a place in the East India Company, which he continued to hold until the company was dissolved. He early began to write, and during his time with the India Company and afterwards gave much time to literature. After he retired from the company in 1858 he devoted himself exclusively to his scientific writing and to politics. He was a member of the House of Commons from 1865–67. During the latter part of his life he lived much in southern France and he died at Avignon in 1873.

J. S. Mill's psychology was presented incidentally. He wrote a *System of Logic* which he based on psychology, he annotated the second edition of his father's *Analysis,* in coöperation with Bain, Findlater, and Grote, and he wrote *An Examination of the Philosophy of Sir William Hamilton.* One must pick out his psychological theory from these works. In general he accepted his father's position and like him analyzed mental phenomena into their simplest parts and made no use of vague faculties or functions. He modified his father's theories mainly by recognizing that they gave an oversimplified description of mind. In the fundamental classification of association he recognized similarity as an independent form, in addition to contiguity in space

and time, and also added intensity and frequency as primary classes. These latter are obviously only factors in producing the association and not new forms of connection.

A second important departure from his father's theories is that the younger Mill thinks of the various elementary sensations and ideas as entering into a very close union when they come together. The elements frequently can no longer be distinguished in the new combination. He explained this loss of identity on the analogy of the formation of new combinations in chemistry. A fusion occurs when muscular sensations blend with visual sensations to form the notion of space that is analogous to the formation of water from hydrogen and oxygen. To understand the development of ideas, we require a chemistry, not merely a physics. The term "mental chemistry" thus suggested by Mill has been frequently present in the literature from his time on.

John Stuart Mill also departed from his father's opinion as to the nature of belief. This he holds to be a type of experience different from the mere presence of a vivid idea or intense sensation. He would accept these as important conditions of belief on certain occasions. Belief is, however, a specific mental attitude, having certain connections with action, since we believe that upon which we are ready to act. He makes no claim for the completeness of his analysis either of the state or of its conditions. Then, too, he would make attention more than the mere dominance of the physically most intense sensation, or of the idea aroused by the strongest associates. Rather the dominance of an idea must be related to the presence of other ideas, themselves pleasant or unpleasant, with which the idea in question becomes associated.

CHAPTER VIII

GERMAN PSYCHOLOGY OF THE EARLY NINE-
TEENTH CENTURY: FRIES, HERBART,
BENEKE, AND LOTZE

THE work in psychology in the early nineteenth century in Germany was a struggle against the rationalizing idealists, the men who were so interested in underlying principles and assumed entities that they had
no place for the concrete. Fichte would turn the universe
into will, Schelling into an indefinite absolute, and
Hegel into idea, but no one of them had any interest
in what the individual consciousness was like or how
human behavior was determined. They did succeed in
carrying the interest of intellectual Germany with them
to such a degree that psychology only gradually received
any notice. Their influence was strong in philosophy
during the first half of the century, and psychology was
largely overlooked. The first to make heard the claims of
an empirical treatment of mind, even feebly, was Fries.

FRIES

Jakob Friedrich Fries was born in Barby in 1773,
became *docent* at Jena in 1801, and was promoted to a

professorship of Philosophy in 1814. In 1819 he was removed from his chair for taking part in a political demonstration at the Wartburg, but was called back as Professor of Mathematics and Physics in 1824, restored to his chair of Philosophy in the following year, and continued to teach until his death in 1843. Fries was interested in the phenomena of mind and endeavored to treat them empirically, although he was highly speculative in his general tendencies. He followed Kant in discussing psychological facts under the head of anthropology, and actually did consider them in the light of the customs of primitive peoples. He is empirical in so far as he thinks of the mental processes themselves as constituting the data that psychology must study. They depend in some way upon a pure ego or self, but this is never known except in its effects. It cannot be appreciated for itself. Fries divides his *Anthropology* into two parts, the mental and the physical. In the first part he studies the actual processes by which we perceive, remember and think. He speaks of faculties and their actions, but at the same time studies the laws that mental states follow. Even in his logic he begins with a description of ideas and of the way they are involved in perception, imagination and thought. In the physical anthropology we find a discussion of the brain and of the relation between brain and mind. He distinguished three main faculties, following Kant, or giving to Kant's division in the critiques a specific differentiation into the faculties of knowledge, feeling and will. He also regarded each faculty as subordinated to or incorporated in the unitary self. Fries is especially important as an evidence that the psychological attitude towards life was surviving in spite of the dominating position of Hegel and Hegelians.

HERBART

The man of the first third of the century who had the most far-reaching and persisting influence upon later psychology, was Johann Friedrich Herbart. Herbart was born in Oldenburg, near Bremen in 1776, entered the University of Jena in 1794, and after receiving his degree tutored in a family at Interlaken, Switzerland, for three years. While there he met Pestalozzi and became so much interested in his system of education that he gave a considerable portion of his later effort to extending it, developing a system of education in general. The first two years of the nineteenth century he spent with friends in Bremen where he devoted himself to the study of philosophy and pedagogy. He became a *docent* at Göttingen in 1802, and was promoted *äusserordentlicher Professor* in 1805. In 1809 he was called to Königsberg as Professor, then returned to Göttingen to the full chair in 1833 and remained until his death in 1841. Herbart had a very wide influence in philosophy and psychology, and a still greater one on education.

He may almost be said to have created theoretical pedagogy. His theories of education were dominant the world over until the beginning of the scientific movement at the opening of the present century and still have weight in certain circles.

Herbart accepted Kant's challenge to make psychology a mathematical science and developed an elaborate system to that end. In addition, he made many careful observations of mental operations, and developed theories on several points that had a wide effect upon later systems. It must be said that while he put most emphasis upon his mathematical constructions they proved much less fruitful than did the other phases of his system. Herbart's general conception of the universe was that it was composed of independent elements, like Leibniz's monads, save that they were not necessarily conscious but were centers of forces and interacted upon each other. He called them *reals*. All things either are or are composed of *reals*. The human soul is one and impressions arise in it when it reacts upon the external world, also made up of *reals*.

Herbart uses the same figure to express the relations of the ideas within mind. Apparently these arise originally from the collision between *reals*, but after he begins his psychological discussion he forgets about the nature of the mind and explains all mental states from an interaction of the ideas. The mind then becomes merely the stage upon which the ideas act, or the space in which they are contained. It makes no real contribution to the action of the mental processes. This shows the difficulty of assuming a real mind and at the same time explaining mental acts in an empirical way. If the mind is to control its acts, no explanation in terms of cause is possible, or at least there is but one cause which explains everything. If one is to explain remembering from earlier connections, then there is no need of mind. The continental philosophers on the whole are content to explain everything from the action of mind, while the English are interested in the interrelations of ideas and ignore mind. Herbart attempted to use both methods. He first developed a system that explained the universe in its relation to mind, with the mind as a true thing and center of activity, in continental fashion, then he neglected this system and explained mental states wholly from the interaction with other mental states within the mind, and from the action of objects upon the senses. He thus combines both systems, although most that was of value belonged to the second.

Unlike the English school, Herbart made his ideas centers of force, that were not merely brought into mind by physiological processes or in some unexplained way, but were always in mind and determined mind by the energies that they themselves possessed. The sensations or ideas, once they come to mind through the senses, are never lost; there is no real forgetting. They continue forever and each contributes to the control of all the others. Even when the individual was not aware of the presence of an idea, it was still an active influence in directing the course of consciousness. Each idea was assumed to have a certain force either positive or negative to which a numerical value was assigned. They acted with these forces very much as heavenly bodies do in gravitation, or as the electrons and protons do in a modern atom. Consciousness also was divided into two parts, consciousness proper and the subconscious. Ideas that seem to be forgotten are merely forced below the threshold of consciousness, because at the moment ideas with signs opposed to their own are too strong for them. When the opposing forces weaken they bob up and are appreciated.

It was in working out the relations between these hypothetical forces that Herbart developed his mathematics. Since the values assigned were purely hypothetical and the relations themselves were not actually observed, the mathematical solutions correspond to nothing real. It was merely a sham mathematical approach. The more general effect was good. Picturing the ideas as determining consciousness by their mutual interaction was new and constituted a valuable means of presenting many psychological facts. Thus attention is explained as due to the action of the ideas in mind upon the sensations that seek to enter. When they are of a character to favor the entrance of sensations of one sort, anything of that class will be noted immediately, all else will be kept out. Entering consciousness meant becoming clear and distinct. Herbart adopted Leibniz's old word "apperception" for the process. To stand out clearly was to be apperceived, and the group of ideas that favored the clearness was called the apperceiving mass. This was one of the first definite recognitions of the influence of earlier experience in determining what shall be noticed, and has been made much of in educational theory from that time to this.

The other concrete mental processes were referred to similar interactions between ideas. Pleasure was felt when there was a mutual coöperation between the separate elements; when there was conflict between them, pain resulted. Pleasure, when attached to a specific object, became a desire. If desire developed at a moment when all else favored movement, action followed. Apperception was thus the determining influence in feeling and will as well as for the more strictly intellectual operations. This treatment derived all mental activities from one set of principles and did away with the necessity for separate faculties. Herbart devoted much space to disproving faculties and to showing that they really did not constitute an explanation of mental processes. This, with his general doctrine of apperception, constituted his most important contribution to psychology.

As has been suggested, Herbart had his most profound influence upon educational theory and practice. From his early acquaintance with Pestalozzi he had himself been interested in the problems of teaching, and his early chairs of teaching combined philosophy and pedagogy. At Königsberg, he started a practice school and applied his doctrines as he developed them. Possibly his most striking theoretical contribution was in showing that what a child will attend to depends upon what he already knows and that he can be prepared to be interested in anything, provided only he have the preliminary knowledge required. This application of the notion of apperception and the name itself was the keystone of educational theory for several generations and is revived still in most systems under other names. In psychology, as in education, Herbart was an outstanding figure, and probably had more influence than any one else from the beginning of the nineteenth century to the rise of experimental psychology under Wundt.

THE FOLK SCHOOL

Herbart had a large school that found representatives until almost the end of the century. One of the striking movements that followed close upon his in time was the school of Folk Psychology, prominent in the fifties and sixties, which sought to explain the development of customs, beliefs, and languages from the primitive to the highest form. Lazarus (1824–1893) wrote a work, *Das Leben der Seele* (*The Life of the Soul*) in which he traced the growth of ethical and other ideals from the most primitive to the highest forms of civilization. Steinthal (1823–1899) performed the same function for language, and applied to it the principles of evolution that were finding their way into Germany. Waitz (1821–1864) developed a more complete anthropology, tracing the psychological laws that governed the rise of customs among the primitive peoples. Steinthal and Lazarus were for a decade the editors of a journal, *Die Zeitschrift für Völkerpsychologie*, which provided a means of publication for the reports of travellers and more theoretical papers that bore on race psychology. On the whole this folk school represented one of the first attempts to develop a systematic anthropology.

BENEKE

A third man who was important for psychology in the first half of the century was Friedrich Eduard Beneke. Beneke was born in Berlin in 1798, studied philosophy and theology there and at Halle, and then became *privat docent* at Berlin. He published a book on the physics of morals in 1824, which offended the authorities who were favorable to Hegel's doctrines, and he was in consequence deprived of his right to teach. This was done over the protest of the faculty who insisted that the removal was opposed to the principle of the freedom of teaching. Hegel himself signed the protest to the Minister of Education, but without avail. Beneke was compelled to transfer to Göttingen where he taught from 1824 to 1827. After Hegel's death he returned to Berlin and held his position there until his own death in 1854.

Beneke's importance for psychology lies chiefly in his insistence on the empirical treatment of the subject and his insistence that metaphysics should rest upon psychology rather than psychology upon metaphysics. Beneke's doctrine is in form a faculty psychology, but his faculties are not self-determining entities or forces, but merely centers of force that react upon each other and upon the stimuli that enter from the world without. As he treats it, the faculty is little more than the capacity of the individual to receive impressions and react upon them. The faculty of seeing is no more than the possibility of receiving impressions through the eye. This ability must be developed through use and through receiving earlier impressions. A blind person who has been given sight would not at first see. Only after light has fallen a number of times upon his eyes would vision develop, and the more frequently the eye is stimulated the more definite becomes the sensation. In this treatment, Beneke represents the same fact that Herbart had ascribed to the action of the apperceiving mass. Beneke ascribed the increasing capacity for perception to the development of a latent faculty, while Herbart referred it to the accumulation of ideas.

Like Herbart and Fries, Beneke assumed that ideas once developed are never lost. We merely cease to be aware of them. They persist as unconscious processes. The return to consciousness is explained as due to the arousal of one faculty by another which has been in the past closely connected with it. Where one faculty is active, the activity will spread from it to those others that have been most closely connected with it or with which it shows the greatest degree of harmony. This retains the fact designated as association, although the causal force is made different. One distinguishes the experience revived in memory or imagination from original perceptions, by reason of the greater vividness or freshness of the latter. Beneke also appreciated the importance of recognition. Here as elsewhere he cites many illuminating instances.

Like Herbart, Beneke too, derives pleasure and pain from the interaction of the conscious elements. Beneke includes the interaction of the original faculty upon the stimulus as well as strains and stresses between the elements themselves. He recognizes five conditions:

1. The stimulus may be too faint for the faculty that receives it. In this case the unfulfillment leads to struggle and so to displeasure.

2. The stimulus may be just adapted to the faculty. This gives indifference and is the usual state in perception.

3. The stimulus may be too strong for the faculty.

This gives rise to a feeling of superfluity and so of pleasure.

4. The stimulus may be slight at first and gradually become too strong. This produces a blunting of the sense.

5. The stimulus may be too strong from the beginning. This is real overstimulation and produces pain.

All the faculties lead naturally to action. Bodily movement, however, is determined by the action of the stimuli upon the faculties. Will is thus the outcome of the mental life as a whole. The work closes with a discussion of the development of mental life and of individual differences. The forms of mental disease are treated in an appendix.

The similarities between Beneke's position and Herbart's led the followers of the latter to assert that Beneke had plagiarized the work of their leader. This he denied, asserting that he had completed the development of his system before he read Herbart. The similarities between the systems lie in the facts observed rather than in the explanations. The emphasis upon the influence of earlier experience upon perception is common to many other writers, as are the derivation of feeling and action from the intellectual processes. The special explanation of each of these facts is sufficiently different in Herbart and in Beneke to make it probable that they were independent developments. Both may be regarded as an outgrowth of the tendency to an empirical attitude.

LOTZE

The last of these German philosophers to make contributions to psychology is Rudolph Hermann Lotze. He lived later than the others and was influenced by advances in the other sciences as they were not; nevertheless he should be treated in this chapter. He like the others, sought to develop a psychology by reasoning from a few general principles what mental life must be. He then confirmed his conclusions by chance observations. Lotze was born at Bautzen in 1817, and entered the University of Leipzig as a student of medicine in 1834. During his student days and later also he was almost as much interested in philosophy as in medicine and attended lectures in both fields. After receiving his degree in medicine, he practised in his home for a year and then began his university work as *docent* in Leipzig in 1839. He succeeded Herbart as Professor of Philosophy at Göttingen in 1844 and remained there until called to Berlin in 1881. He died before the end of the year. The burghers of Göttingen hinted that it was of a broken heart at leaving their "gemüthliche Stadt."

Lotze lectured on all branches of philosophy, including psychology. His most important psychological work was his *Medicinische Psychologie* (*Medical Psychology*) published in 1852. In this the influence of his medical training is clearly seen, although it is subordinated to his philosophy. He believes that the results of thinking last longer than the results of investigation. He asserts in one place that the beautiful theories of the nature of the nerves and of their action will be supplanted in half a dozen years by others, equally pretty but entirely different. In philosophy he was a realist, believing in a real mind and an actual external world that react upon each other through a substantial brain. The mind was put in the base of the cerebrum where the fibers entering on the way to the cortex come close together. Exactly how mind might produce an effect upon brain or brain upon mind could not be pictured clearly. Notwithstanding the difficulties in picturing the action of the mind upon the brain, he points out that they are no greater than the difficulties attached to understanding how any physical effect is produced. One knows almost as much about how the mind is affected by a physical stimulus as one does about how heat causes a solid to expand, or about any other familiar purely physical interrelation.

Probably the most lasting contribution that Lotze made to psychology was his doctrine of local signs, which constituted an explanation of how we perceive space. This grew out of his picture of the relation of mind and body. If the mind is in the center of the cerebrum, and has no knowledge of the surface of the body or of the

retina except through the nerves that lead from the surface, it becomes a question how it can know where each stimulus comes from. The mind would be like a telephone operator in the central office receiving messages from all about the town, but with no knowledge where the other end of the wire might be. Lotze suggested that the sensation from each point on the skin or eye had a quality peculiar to itself that led to its reference to the correct point. It would be as if the telephone operator in our figure knew the voice of each subscriber and the subscriber were forbidden to use any but his own instrument. For sight, the quality that characterized each point was determined by the sensitivity of the point on the retina to the color, by the clearness of the impression, and by the movement necessary to bring the fovea to receive the impression from that point. On the skin, the quality varies with the thickness of the membrane, its degree of tension and the underlying fat. This sign indicates how to move the finger to touch it, or evokes the visual picture of the point on the skin. All these signs together serve to develop a notion of position and extent, that is in slight degree present in the individual at birth.

Lotze's *Medicinische Psychologie* covers a wide range, from the nature of the soul, through the mental stages of animals and their instincts, to a description of mental diseases. Mention may be made of the full treatment that is given of the bodily accompaniments of the emotions. All the circulatory and respiratory processes are enumerated as fully as could be expected from common observation unaided by experiment, and many glandular changes are noted. Lotze did not, however, anticipate the James-Lange theory, since he regarded the emotion as the cause of the bodily state and did not look upon the bodily response as the determinant of the emotion.

Considering that the work was written after Johannes Müller had done much of his work, and Helmholtz had begun his, the treatment of anatomical and physiological knowledge is not so full as it might have been. The general psychology, based on introspection, was a marked contribution, and the whole spirit of the work tended to further the development of empirical psychology. For a considerable period after his death, Lotze had a marked influence upon the development of psychology in Germany, and had several loyal students in America who spread his fame and his contributions there. His was a system in which *a priori* deduction and scientific observation met, but in which the rational element dominated. The experimental attack on these problems had been begun in his later years and was soon to replace the older method.

CHAPTER IX

GERMAN PHYSIOLOGY AND EXPERIMENTAL PSYCHOLOGY—JOHANNES MÜLLER

MODERN scientific psychology is an outgrowth of many sciences. Up to the present we have been tracing the somewhat tangled thread of speculation concerning mind, together with direct observation of mental states, from which one side of modern psychology developed. Almost as much of what is recognized today as psychology grew out of the work of the separate sciences, especially from the results of the physiologists. The development of modern experimental science from the mystic interpretations of life and matter that were the work of the alchemists and astrologists of the middle ages was very slow. Paracelsus and van Helmont did much to improve medical theories, but nevertheless both believed in the effect of the heavenly bodies upon man's physical processes and in the action at a distance of various agencies. We have seen how slowly the belief in animal spirits gave way to a physical and chemical interpretation of nervous action. Progress was similarly slow in other connections.

Now and again, even in the middle ages, men like

Leonardo da Vinci, Sylvius, Vesalius, and later Galileo, Kepler, or Newton would make an experiment or collect observations that would profoundly change the course of thought in some one field, but these single advances would be followed by long periods in which no further progress was made. It was not until the eighteenth century that there was anything like a continuous advance, and not until the early decades of the nineteenth that regular systematic work upon scientific problems was begun. Then only do we find persistent and well coördinated experimental attack upon all fronts of human ignorance. All the western nations, but particularly England, France, and Germany, contributed to this advance. In chemistry and physics, Priestley in England, Franklin, and Lavoisier in France made many discoveries in the later eighteenth century that stimulated general progress. Albrecht von Haller, professor in the University of Göttingen from 1736 to 1777, was responsible in large part for a change in attitude towards vital functions which made them chemical and physical processes rather than the result of mystic or anthropomorphic forces. He did much to advance a knowledge of circulation and respiration in connection with nervous action. It was not until the nineteenth century, however, that the fruits of scientific work became completely apparent. Then nearly every university had men who were conducting investigations and their united efforts effected great advances. Johannes Müller was typical of this group of men. He both made many contributions himself and coördinated the work of others.

JOHANNES MÜLLER

Johannes Müller lived the quiet life of the typical German scholar. Born at Coblenz in 1801, he was a student at Bonn and Berlin. At the end of his student days he became *docent* at Bonn, and was promoted through the various ranks to the Professorship of Anatomy and Physiology in 1830. In 1833 he was called to Berlin to the first chair established in Germany for physiology alone. Before that, all such chairs had included anatomy and physiology. As a physiologist, Müller considered that his subject included all functions of the human being, thought and voluntary action as well as body processes. In fact, almost all the topics now covered by psychology were dealt with in his *Handbuch der Physiologie des Menschens,* first published in Coblenz in 1833 (*Elements of Physiology,* London, 1838).

Müller contributed to the advance in psychology by giving new ideas of the action of the nervous system, by studying sensation, especially vision, by observations on retention and recall of impressions and by general theories of the nature of life and mind. His recognition of the sensori-motor nature of all action was the forerunner of much modern work and may be regarded as anticipating the present interpretation of movement as ideo-motor and of mental processes in terms of stimulus and response. Müller was led to this opinion by the discoveries of Bell and Magendie that the posterior roots of the spinal cord contained sensory, and the anterior roots, motor nerves. Hall had already concluded from this and his own observations that action in the cord was a reflex, in which the stimulus went over the posterior nerve and excited the muscle over the anterior nerve. Müller confirmed this theory by more accurate experiment and extended the notion to include all action, of the brain as well as the cord. In voluntary action the sensory impulse is carried to the brain, and there the mind controls the course that the motor impulse shall take, but still it is essentially an act in response to the stimulus.

To the question of sensation, Müller's most lasting contribution was his so-called doctrine of "specific energy of nerve." By this he meant that a given nerve almost always responds in the same way, no matter what the physical stimulus may be that excites it. Thus a "cold spot" on the skin always gives the sensation of cold whether it be stimulated by a cold object, by a hot object, by an electric current, or by physical contact. This means that the quality of a sensation does not depend upon the nature of the object in the external world but upon the nerve itself. Later investigation showed that the nerve fibre was probably indifferent in its response and that the peculiar quality depended

either upon the sense organ or upon the part of the
brain with which it was connected. Müller considered
the second possibility, but not the former. This doctrine has been modified in detail but still, in its essentials, stands as one of the fundamental doctrines of
sense physiology and psychology.

In perception, Müller did many experiments upon
the problems of visual space. One of his first works
was devoted to the question of how it is that we see but
a single object in spite of having an impression of it
from each eye. He found his answer in the fact that the
nerves from the same half of each retina went to the
one part of the brain, and thus he thought the two
images were received by a single nerve element. He also
worked out the positions that objects must occupy in
space if they are to give rise to a single image. He
showed that if the eyes converge upon a point near the
eyes and midway between them, only objects that lie
upon a circle which passes through the point of fixation and the nodal points of the two eyes will be seen as
one. All others are seen double. This circle he called
the horopter circle. Wheatstone had studied the influence of double images in the perception of depth and
had, unknown to Müller, devised his stereoscope. The
two discoveries prepared the way for Helmholtz's development of the knowledge of the perception of depth.
In his theory of space Müller was a follower of Kant
in assuming that we were born with a notion of extent,

and needed experience only to determine how the extended surfaces were to be filled.

Müller devotes a relatively long book to the mind. He pictures mind in general after the fashion of Aristotle. It is the form or entelechy of the body. All living things have a vital principle that moulds their bodily growth according to the idea implied in that species. This "form" passes from the parent to the offspring at the time of fertilization and lasts as long as the race. It determines that the physiological processes shall give each part the shape peculiar to the animal. This mystic "vital force" became the center of a bitter controversy, and finally Helmholtz, Maier, and others substituted for it the principle of conservation of energy, which affirmed that all energy is derived from other energy, that energy is neither lost nor gained in the universe, and that the chemical and physical forces are sufficient to explain all living as well as non-living activities. Mind in man was but one expression of this idea or form that rules the whole of the organism. The vital principle was spread throughout all tissues, but only that part of it which was connected with the brain could give rise to or be the seat of clear ideas.

In his detailed explanation of mental processes, Müller made an original observation of memory after-images, or primary memory images, that is still often quoted. He noticed while lying awake at night after a long day with the microscope, that he would frequently see the tissues he had studied during the day in their full sensory vividness, as if they were still before him. These persistent images must, he says, have a physiological basis, but he was not ready to assign them to any special part of the brain. These ideas, that are retained in the brain, are revived through association. Similarity and coexistence are recognized as forms of association. In addition to the more restricted associations, however, one must account for the fact that one selects from the potential associates only certain ones. This selection he explains much after the manner of Herbart as due to the other ideas that are latent, but still exert an influence upon the course of thought. Müller anticipates Galton in making an abstract idea a precipitate from numerous concrete ones, in which common elements are retained and the rest drop out. This common remnant constitutes the notion or its representatives in mind.

Feelings were explained by Müller, as by Aristotle and Herbart, as due to harmonious combination or opposition between ideas. Pain arises when striving is thwarted by counter-striving, and pleasure is felt when there is free activity, especially when there is free activity after earlier restraint. Emotions are discussed with reference to the bodily sensations that accompany them, and are then given a formal classification on the pattern of Spinoza. Action is said to be due to the direction of the nervous processes by ideas. A given sensation or idea becomes connected with a movement by a series of responses, made at first without intention. When the connection is established it can be controlled by will. He indicates that the attending circumstances, including the accompanying feelings and the necessity for the act, influence the course of the act. Will is also shown to be connected with attention. Both are controlled in much the same way and have many elements in common. We may make movements involuntarily when the idea is present with no intention of moving. This is seen in the gestures accompanying speech and elsewhere.

Müller's contributions to psychology thus are varied. His influence was very great, both in setting a fashion for the investigation of sensory processes, which led many of his successors to continue that work, and in his specific contributions on these many problems. It prepared the way for a physiological psychology, which the interests of Wundt chanced to make more psychology than physiology. One can imagine that, had it been taken up with a slightly more biological interest, a psychological physiology, rather than a physiological psychology, would have developed.

WEBER

A second German physiologist, a contemporary of Müller, who has given his name to one of the best known laws of psychology, was Ernst Heinrich Weber. Weber was born in Wittenberg in 1795, became *docent* at Leipzig in 1817, was appointed assistant professor the following year, and received the full chair in 1821. He continued his work until 1871 and died in 1878. One of his brothers was professor of physics at Göttingen and another professor of physiology at Halle. They worked together on certain problems. For example, the physicist developed electrical apparatus, which Ernst Heinrich used in showing the nervous control of the heart.

Weber's most famous contribution to psychology came from his demonstration that the least noticeable difference between two sensation intensities was always proportional to the original intensity being dealt with. Thus he found that when he lifted a weight of 32 ounces, he could notice the addition of one ounce, and when he lifted four ounces the just noticeable difference was approximately one-eighth of an ounce. The fraction of the original that must be added to make a second weight noticeably different from the first, varied for different individuals from $\frac{1}{30}$ to $\frac{1}{50}$. When the weight was not lifted but merely rested upon the skin, $\frac{1}{3}$ of the original must be added if a difference were to be detected. Weber urged this as evidence that the muscles were more sensitive than the skin, and that there was a true muscle sense. Weber also tested the capacity to discriminate lengths of lines, and found that the average individual detected differences of about $\frac{1}{50}$. This fraction he assumed to be constant for all intensities of sensations and for all lengths of lines. What we now know as the fraction of Weber's Law is the direct measure of sensitivity.

A second well-known experiment made by Weber was determining the accuracy with which points on the skin can be realized to be distinct. Weber showed that if touched upon the finger-tips with blunt pointed compasses, the subject would feel the two points as two when the contacts were a millimeter apart, whereas if touched upon the back of the finger, the points must be forty to sixty millimeters apart to be so felt. Points nearer together than these were felt as one. This fact suggested Lotze's theory of local signs, and has served as the factual basis for many theories of space. These two contributions of Weber have received much attention from later psychology, so that Weber's name is very familiar to the student—more familiar, in fact, than Müller's name, although Müller made more contributions of a theoretical character and was much more what we should call psychologically minded than Weber.

VON HELMHOLTZ

The great Herman von Helmholtz, possibly the last man to deserve the name of universal scientist, is also to be counted among the important contributors to psychology. Helmholtz was born in Potsdam, in 1821, the son of a *Gymnasium* teacher. In 1838, he entered the special school for the training of military surgeons in Berlin, where he studied for five years. As the rules of the school prescribed that in return for their education graduates must spend a period as military surgeon, he served with the troops at Potsdam for five years. He then became instructor in anatomy in an art school at Berlin, and was appointed professor of anatomy and physiology at Königsberg, where he remained until 1855. Later he was professor in the same subjects at Bonn and Heidelberg, successively. His work on the stimulation of nerves had led him to investigate electrical phenomena for themselves, and his work in the physiology of sight and hearing forced him to study sound and light as physical forces, so that he was as well known for his work in physics as in physiology. Thus it came that he was called to Berlin as professor of physics in 1871, where he continued his work until his death, which occurred on his return trip from the Chicago Columbian Exposition in 1894.

Helmholtz's early work was on the action of muscle and nerve. Possibly his most striking contribution to the field was the measurement of the rate of propagation of the nerve impulse, shortly after Müller had asserted that it was instantaneous, or at least required a time much too short to be measured. His first work that bore more directly upon psychological problems was the study of the various mechanisms of the eye. He invented the opthalmoscope for the direct observation of the retina, measured the optical constants of the eye completely and accurately, showed how the lens accommodates the eye for different distances, and put all these facts together into a theory of visual space. These studies were first published separately and then were brought together in his *Handbook of Physiological Optics* in 1861. It is interesting to note that this work in a revised form was thought worthy of translation into English in 1924, more than sixty years after its original publication.

In the matter of space, Helmholtz adopted a definitely empirical position. He believes that the child is born with very slight capacity for the perception of space and learns how to appreciate position, length and distance. He extended the experiments of Müller to determine the nature of the horopter, and developed a mathematical proof for its form. He developed the experiments of Wheatstone on the function of double images in the perception of depth, and in general collected and interpreted the work of his predecessors and contemporaries in the field of space perception. His most characteristic conclusion is that we perceive spatial relations by a process of "unconscious inference." We have learned that certain peculiarities of an experience constitute a sign that the object is to be found at a given distance. We infer how far away it must be on the basis of these signs, without even being aware that we have noticed the sign itself. Thus a definite degree of doubleness of an image is interpreted to mean that it is two feet nearer than the object we are looking at. We see it as two feet nearer immediately, but do not notice that the image is double at all.

Helmholtz's color theory was also an important contribution to psychology. He accepted the general principles of a theory devised by Thomas Young, an English physicist. In essentials this theory assumes that the sensations we receive through the eye may be reduced to three primary qualities and that the others are developed by combining these three in different ways. The three primary colors are determined by three distinct kinds of organs in the eye, which when stimulated give rise to red, green, and violet. When red and green are stimulated, yellow results, and other colors are produced by combining the stimulation of other pairs. When all three organs are excited at once, white is seen. A color-blind man lacks one or two of the organs, either red or green or red and green. After-images are due to looking at a white surface after one of the organs has been fatigued so that we see with the unfatigued organs alone. Contrast, by which we mean that a colored surface induces its complement on a neighboring surface, was explained as an error in judgment. This theory has been modified and extended by various students of Helmholtz in the light of more recent discoveries, and in its revised form must be regarded as one of the three important contemporary theories.

Helmholtz has quite as important a place in the realm of sound as in that of sight. He studied carefully the structure of the ear, and developed a notion of its mechanics that is still accepted by many, if not by everyone, to this day. The so-called resonance theory of hearing he propounded in his *Tonlehre,* published in 1862 and in several later editions (translated by Havelock Ellis as *Sensations of Tone*). This theory assumes that the basilar membrane is the resolving organ of hearing; that it is made up of a series of fibres of different lengths, each of which is tuned to some one of the audible notes. When the vibrations of corresponding rate are carried to the liquid of the inner ear, the string that is tuned to it is excited by resonance and this arouses the nerve fibre connected with it which in turn gives rise to the tone in the cortex. Helmholtz also developed a theory of musical consonance which assumes that pleasant notes are those that do not beat either in themselves or between their overtones, while all unpleasant or dissonant combinations do beat.

It will be seen that Helmholtz was an important influence in developing the psychology and physiology of sensation and perception, and well deserves a place in a history of the growth of psychology.

HERING

Another physiologist, who wrote on most of the topics treated by Helmholtz which bear on psychology, was Ewald Hering. Hering was born at Altersdorf, Saxony, in 1834, studied at the University of Leipzig and became *docent* there in 1862. He went to Vienna as professor in a church medical school in 1865, was called to the chair of physiology at Prague in 1870 and to Leipzig in 1895. He died in 1918, two years after his retirement.

Hering attracted attention in 1870 by a paper he presented before the Vienna Academy entitled "On Memory as a Function of Organized Matter." In this paper he held that retention is to be looked upon as a general expression of the fact that any operation that has once been performed is more easily performed upon repetition. He cited as instances the ease with which a nail may be driven a second time in the same spot, the scriptural reference to the bending of a twig, and the learning through practice to use a muscle. We may assume, he says, that the change made in the brain by the passage of a nerve process in perception has an entirely analogous explanation. A second time it tends to follow the same path, and we call this memory. The paper was much used by James and others, and was translated into English some years after its first publication.

Hering had a very well developed color theory which differed from that of Helmholtz in almost every point. He assumed that we must have four primary colors rather than three, and gave evidence to show that yellow was an independent color and not a combination of red and green as Helmholtz believed. His fundamental principle was that colors occur in pairs and that each pair, rather than each color, has a single organ. The complementary colors, red and green and blue and yellow, are opposite ways of responding in a single organ. Green corresponds to a building up or anabolic process in the organ, and red to a destructive or catabolic process. Blue is the anabolic, yellow the catabolic process. When two complementary colors fall upon the retina at the same time and place, the upbuilding and destructive processes cancel each other and no color is seen. Hering assumed that there was an independent organ that was stimulated by all light to give white, and which when it recovered from stimulation gave rise to black. When the colors cancelled each other this second excitation was alone present and white was seen. Negative after-images were explained as due to recovery from the earlier stimulation. Anabolism followed catabolism and excessive building up due to stimulation by green or blue was followed by return to the normal, which was, relatively, catabolism. Color-blindness was due to the absence of the red-green organ, and on this theory one could not be blind to one color of the pair alone. In fact it is rare to have blindness to one color of the pair with vision for the other, and Hering's partisans doubt if it ever happens. The Helmholtz and Hering theories still dispute the field, save for the appearance of Mrs. Ladd-Franklin's theory which is in some measure a compromise between them. Later results, especially the discovery that rods and cones have different functions, agree with neither of them completely, but have been remodelled to meet them. Whether either theory has triumphed, and which more nearly meets the facts, is still a topic of bitter controversy.

Hering also applied his notion of the opposed processes of anabolism and catabolism to explain the sensations of heat and cold. Warm sensations were asserted to be due to catabolism in the common organ, cold to anabolism. This theory was automatically disproved when Donaldson and others showed that warmth and cold were appreciated by different spots on the skin.

Hering also challenged vigorously Helmholtz's notion that space was built up empirically. He insisted that one can see no resemblance between space and sensations of strain or the other sensations that Helmholtz said entered into its composition. We must assume that space is an original possession of the mind. He even denied that we could learn to combine corresponding points to give a single image. These must depend upon original anatomical connections, and the ideas of distance that are connected with them must have been joined to them at birth and could not have been associated with them through experience. Helmholtz has probably been given the better of this argument by later opinion, although agreement on the main problem is by no means universal.

OTHER PHYSIOLOGISTS

These four men constitute only representatives of a very large number of physiologists who have worked on psychological problems from the beginning of last century. The list could be greatly extended. Purkinje was one of the early men who did much to develop a knowledge of the eye and its appendages and made a number of important observations on color sensations. One might also mention Sigmund Exner, born in Vienna in 1846 and professor of physiology in the University there since 1875, as a physiologist who has contributed to the advancement of psychological knowledge. He was one of the first to measure the time required for reaction to a simple stimulus; his investigations of the visual perception of motion were those of a pioneer and the results still stand. Possibly his most important contribution for the time was a study of the localization of cerebral functions, and the development of a theory of the physiological basis of mental acts. It was highly important when published, and in spite of advances in knowledge since is still well worth reading.

How close was the relation between psychology and physiology even in comparatively recent times is seen from the list of editors of the second of the great psychological journals founded in Germany, the *Zeitschrift für die Psychologie und die Physiologie der Sinnesorganen,* which began publication in 1890. The editors were Ebbinghaus and König, the former a psychologist, the latter a physicist who had worked with Helmholtz on vision. The coöperating board consisted of Aubert, Exner, Helmholtz, Hering, von Kries, Lipps, G. E. Müller, Preyer and Stumpf. Of these only the last four were psychologists, the others were physiologists and physicists. In the list of physiologists von Kries deserves mention for his work on sensation, especially the sensations of sight. He was one of the three men to revise Helmholtz's *Physiological Optics* in 1910, and published numerous works of his own.

CHAPTER X

THE FOUNDING OF EXPERIMENTAL PSYCHOLOGY
—FECHNER AND WUNDT

WHILE its beginnings were most closely connected with physiology, the physicists also contributed towards the growth of psychology. One of these in the last generation was Mach. But the outstanding figure of the earlier period who brought physical methods and physical knowledge to bear on psychological problems was Gustave Theodore Fechner.

FECHNER

Fechner was one of the picturesque characters of the last century in Germany. Originally a physicist, he varied his early work with mystical speculations, with aesthetics, with investigations in psychology, and lightened it with humorous writings. At the end he left an impression as a psychologist rather than as a physicist.

Fechner was born in the Wendish country near Muskau in 1801. His father, a village preacher, died when the son was five years old, but not before he had taught him to speak Latin as well as he did German. Fechner entered the University of Leipzig in 1817 and

GROUP OF PSYCHOLOGISTS AT THE CELEBRATION OF WUNDT'S 80TH
BIRTHDAY

maintained his connection with the university for seventy years. He first studied medicine, but soon found he was not interested and turned to mathematics and metaphysics. Although he received his M.D., he never practiced medicine. Instead he took up physics and we find him in 1824 taking over the lectures in that subject, and beginning a period of laboratory investigation. He reached the rank of professor in 1834. His resources were so slight in the early years of his academic life that he undertook a large amount of literary work to supplement them. He edited and in large part wrote an encyclopedia of household knowledge in eight volumes; he edited a pharmaceutical journal and translated a number of books on physics from the French, aside from conducting his own investigations and teaching. He broke under the strain and became a nervous invalid. His eyes were hypersensitive to light, so that he could not leave the house without a bandage over them, and all the rest of his life he was limited to a few hours' reading a day.

For a number of years he struggled on, teaching when he was able, but for the most part trying to regain his health. In 1844 he gave up, was retired on a small stipend as emeritus, and lectured only as he felt inclined, and then mostly on philosophical and psychological topics. He lived an invalid for forty-three years, and in spite of his ill health was a productive scholar during all that period. He published even in the last of his eighty-six years. His was an interesting case for the neurologist. It might be in line with a recent clinical style in biography—and while not offered with great seriousness, it would surely prove no worse than many—to treat his disease as a neurosis developed as a defence mechanism. It appears that he was either unwilling or unable to learn the mathematics required if he was to do much in physics. One might suggest that he developed an inferiority complex on this account, or in terms of another system, that he took flight from reality, and found an excuse for himself in blindness and accompanying symptoms.

Fechner's first and greatest psychological book was his *Elemente der Psychophysik*, published in 1860 and reprinted by Wundt in 1889, two years after Fechner's death. In this he published the results of his exhaustive experiments upon the measurement of sensation. He reports that he was led to these experiments with the definite purpose of finding a means of measuring sensation. He says that he was lying awake one morning when the idea came to him that what was needed for measuring mental processes was a unit, and that this unit might be supplied by the least noticeable difference between two sensation intensities. It is always possible to say whether a sensation is or is not present, and it is also possible to say when one sensation is just noticeably greater than another. These two determinable points are all that is necessary to construct a scale. If one determines the sensation intensity that can just be appreciated, and then the intensity of a stimulus giving a sensation just noticeably greater than that, one has the first unit. If one will determine the entire number of sensations that can just be discriminated between the faintest and any given stimulus, one will have the measure of that sensation. This just noticeable difference between two sensations was to be for sensation what the millimeter is for distance. With this idea in mind, Fechner made very careful measurements of the discrimination of each of the senses by methods that he had himself devised. These results, and even more the methods, were of great value but the original problem remained unsolved. The difficulty proved to be that one cannot use the determination of one experiment for the next. The limen, or faintest stimulus that can just be perceived, varies from day to day and each of the just noticeably different stimuli varies also. There is no way of knowing where one left off the day before, no way of marking the stimulus or sensation obtained one day so that it may be secured again the day after. Fechner confirmed Weber's Law and determined the limits within which it applied. He formulated the law in the statement that the sensation varies as the logarithm of the stimulus, and saw in it an expression of the relation of body and mind.

In addition to the extended treatment of sensation intensities and their relation to stimuli, which he called the outer psychophysics, Fechner discussed in his second volume what he called the inner psychophysics. Under this head he treats of the differences between sleep and waking, and, what had a wider influence, of the stages that separate sensation from memory. He asserted that sensations always leave after-images, and that they also leave more subjective after-effects that resemble the original very closely. These he called the memory after-images. They persist for some seconds in an intensity but slightly less than the original and then in most individuals vanish very quickly. Unlike after-images, too, they do not depend in strength upon the time of fixation; a brief but attentive glance gives just as strong a memory after-image as longer fixation. Memory images, the third stage, return after having been out of consciousness for a longer or shorter period. These in Fechner's own experience were relatively faint and uncertain in outline, although he took a census of the memory images of distinguished men which indicated that for others they might approach the vividness of actual sensations.

Fechner spent a large part of the remainder of his life replying to criticism of his theory of psychophysics. These turned mostly upon the interpretation that should be given the observed facts, although Hering thought the law as a whole had little validity. The experiments themselves were recognized by all as a monument to his patience, and the methods have proved fundamental for many investigations in the most varied fields. The wider inferences that Fechner would draw from them have lost much in interest as other problems have come to the fore, and greater knowledge of the nervous system puts a new interpretation upon them.

In 1876 he published a two volume work, *Die Vorschule der Aesthetik*, in which he developed methods for investigating beauty experimentally. He carried out a large number of experiments to determine the most beautiful combination of lines and arrangements of parts of a simple figure. Among these were the best proportions of the parts of a cross to one another, the most pleasing oval and rectangle. He then attempted to confirm these experiments by studying the types of figures that were actually used by great artists in their paintings. The book was an important production and a remarkable one for a man of seventy-five.

In his more general philosophy Fechner was a mystic and a panpsychic with an oriental strain. One of his works, *Zend Avesta*, endows all things with personal souls. Another on the same line was *Nanna*, or a study of plant souls. He thought of the human soul as related to the body as the inside of a circle is related to the outside. As with Spinoza, body and soul were different aspects of the same fundamental unity. In this connection, Fechner looked upon his formula for Weber's Law as a corollary of the relation between body and mind. The stronger stimuli lost more of themselves in the passage from the physical to the mental world. Weber's Law was the result of the greater loss, for what was left to reach the realm of sensation was relatively the same for all intensities, but absolutely much less than for the fainter stimuli. This loss may be looked upon as the toll paid by a physical stimulus for the privilege of entering the better realm of the soul.

Fechner stands as one of the most picturesque characters in the history of psychology. To have covered the range from physics to philosophy in his serious work, and to have kept the pot boiling by undertakings which variously won him recognition, as author of a household encyclopedia and as a recognized humorist, was no mean achievement. This is all the more remarkable when we think that he was officially declared a hopeless invalid at forty-two, and then lived on to eighty-six with no single year in which he did not make a serious contribution to the work he was most interested in. Fechner was the first to give psychology a definite experimental foundation, and his contributions, and especially the methods he devised, still stand, even if we accept the judgment of his harshest critics as to the interpretation that should be put upon them. He was truly the founder of experimental psychology.

WUNDT

Wilhelm Wundt may be said to share with Fechner the honor of founding experimental psychology. If he did not actually originate the experimental method, he at least did much to extend it, established the first laboratory specifically devoted to psychology, founded the first periodical for the publication of experimental investigations, and generally consolidated the position of psychology as an experimental science. Wundt was born at Neckerau in Baden in 1832. He was a student of medicine and philosophy at Tübingen, 1851–55, and later at Heidelberg where he received his degrees; he became assistant in the medical clinic at Heidelberg University in 1856, *docent* in 1857, full professor in 1864. He was also made assistant to Helmholtz in 1871, and it is said that he was discouraged from going into physiology because Helmholtz thought he did not know enough mathematics. He was appointed professor of philosophy at Zurich in 1873, and the following year returned to Germany as professor of philosophy at Leipzig where his real career began. He conducted experiments in psychology in his own dwelling at first, and was given an official laboratory in 1879, the first in the world.

Wundt soon reached a position of preëminence in the psychological world that was challenged by few. His position was due to his enthusiasm, which attracted large numbers of students from all parts of the world and urged them to many important investigations, to his originality in theoretical construction, and still more to his ability to collect and organize the work of

others in the field. The men who were to be the leaders
of psychology in several countries began to flock to
Leipzig and carried the methods and incentives to new
work back to their home lands. Cattell, Hall, and many
others from America were among the first students.
Bourdon and Henri, from France, came in a later group,
and not a few Germans aided in spreading the influence
and the methods of Wundt by later accepting places in
other countries.

Wundt's writings were encyclopedic, and, if we are to
measure accomplishment mechanically by number of
pages, few men have produced so much. In 1863 appeared the *Sinneswahrnehmungen* (Sense Perceptions)
that was largely a summary of the work already done
in sensation. The *Grundzüge der physiologischen Psychologie* (Outlines of Physiological Psychology) was
first published in 1874, and was revised five times,
the final sixth edition, printed in 1908–1911, being
in three volumes and containing nearly 2400 pages.
Wundt brought out several more popular works and
text-books in psychology from time to time. Finally in
1900, when nearly seventy years old, he began to
write his *Völkerpsychologie* (Folk Psychology) that
was finally extended to ten large volumes. Some of
these volumes were revised for second editions before
the whole was finished. To these must be added a
System der Philosophie, an *Ethics* and a *Logic* in two
volumes. In his early years he published three works

of importance on physiology. Good health, a marvellously regular routine and a long life made possible this great output, which, if of uneven value, was all respectable and was certainly imposing in mass.

As Wundt may be said to have given the first definite systematization of the material of psychology, at least in Germany, it may be well to give a brief summary of the contents of his *Physiological Psychology*. He began with an extended treatment of the nervous system, then turned to a very full review of what was known of sensation, including an elaborate description of the sense organs. He made sensation and feeling the elements of mind, treating them as the modern structuralists do. Sensations were discussed under the head of the four attributes, intensity, quality, extent and duration, a method of treatment which Wundt introduced. Under intensity he reviewed the work in psychophysics with the theories of Weber's Law. Under quality he discussed the more general facts of sensation. Extent and duration were put over for later discussion under perception.

Feeling was made equally fundamental with sensation, as an immediately known element of consciousness. Two qualities of feeling, pleasure and pain, were distinguished in the first editions, but in the fifth, which appeared in 1902, Wundt added two pairs of qualities: strain and relaxation, and exhilaration and depression. In addition he asserted that the quality of feeling varied in some degree with each different sensation, but did not attempt to enumerate these qualities or say definitely how the variations were related to the differences in sensation qualities. In his theory of feeling he showed that the quality was dependent upon the reaction of apperception to the stimulus. When the response is easy there is pleasure, when there is too much conflict, pain.

Next followed a discussion of ideas, which was made to include the representations of external objects, either in perception or in memory. He discussed first the perceptions, which were regarded as combinations of sensations and memories, so closely blended that there was no possibility of drawing a sharp line between the two. He grouped ideas, according to attributes, as intensive ideas, space ideas and time ideas. Under the first he discussed consonance and dissonance and other musical combinations; under the two latter, the general facts and theories of space and time. Space he treated as partly innate, so far as it was dependent upon inherited nervous connections, and partly empirical, for much depends upon the organization of movements and ideas. He regarded the muscular movements as an essential element in all space ideas, and made much use of the eye-muscles in explaining optical illusions and the learning of the appreciation of distance. The perception of time gave a summary of what was known about temporal appreciation and the rhythmic processes connected with it, and a discussion of the nature of rhythm itself.

Under emotions Wundt gave the most important place to a discussion of the aesthetic processes. He included in this section a statement of what was known about bodily changes during the emotions, but on the whole was more interested in determining the primary feeling and sensational content of the emotions than the bodily changes that accompanied or might be regarded as inducing them. Actions are derived from emotions, for no act and no decision is made unless some emotion be present. All forms of action may be developed from the simple impulse in which the initiating process is a feeling without idea. As ideas come in to direct the movement we have volitional action, and then, with deliberate selection of one of two ends, we have choice.

Probably the most characteristic feature of the Wundtian psychology centers about his notion of apperception. In this he combines the meanings that had been given the term by Leibniz and Herbart, and then supplies a physiological mechanism for it. As with Leibniz, apperception is marked empirically by the clearness of consciousness. Consciousness at any moment is like the field of vision with a clear point in the center and a field of increasing vagueness as it departs from that point. This focus is known as the point of apperception. Apperception is also used as the cause of the clearness of the field of consciousness. Taken as a whole, this use is practically synonymous with will. It is the cause of attending, and attention to the idea of a movement causes that movement actually to take place. So, indirectly, apperception is the final term in causing action. When, however, one attempts to find the conditions for apperception, one must look to the ideational processes dominant at the moment and their relations to the stimuli and to each other. It is not clear how far Wundt would go in the reduction of apperception to these ideational influences. He asserts that the great error in Herbart's psychology is exclusive reference of all other processes to ideas, and usually apperception or will is spoken of as a single force or unit without reduction. But he does state that the course of apperception is determined by the ideas and feelings already present.

Apperception was given a definite nervous seat in the frontal lobes of the brain. It is there that the association fibres run from all the sensory and motor areas. We can think of it as the coördinating center for all the sensory and motor processes. Whether apperception is to be regarded as the expression of this interaction or as a fundamental force that controls the rest of the cortex from this seat, is again not made clear. This process with a definite bodily seat also has a definite conscious sign in the feeling of activity or strain sensations that accompany its functioning. These, too, seem at times to be regarded as real causes of changes in

body or ideas and not mere accompaniments. Whatever it may be in essence, apperception is, according to Wundt, the central force in the explanation of the mental processes.

Association is, somewhat grudgingly and with reservations, made the basis of the processes of recall. The classifications of associations are manifold and complicated. First there are groupings according to the product. Sensations unite with one another to form ideas, and then association also explains the recall of ideas. Each form has several subdivisions. Combinations of sensations alone are called fusions, combinations of sensations with memory images are called assimilations. In recall, we have the associations of the external type, due to the ordinary contiguity and succession of original occurrence, and to similarity; and internal connections, determined by the meanings of the ideas. All recall is controlled by apperception as well as by association. Association is fundamental here, in the sense that there must have been association to make possible the recall. Apperception selects from the possible associates those which are in accord with the entire past of the individual as well as with the single connection. In this again the mass of experience seems at times to be regarded as itself the cause, and apperception is but a name for the process.

Wundt regarded mind and body as relatively distinct, but still closely connected, entities. There is no causal relation between them, but merely a psychophysical parallelism. The two series of processes keep step in some mysterious way, but neither causes the action of the other. This is similar to the occasionalism of Geulincx and to the preëstablished harmony of Leibniz, but makes use of no metaphysical explanation of what keeps the two series in step.

Wundt's most important influence on psychology was in giving it an experimental turn. His ideal was to confirm each statement by experiment, and to rely upon proved fact as the real datum of the science. Many different types of experiments were carried out by himself and his students. He continued the work of the physiologists on the qualities of sensation and that of Fechner on the intensity relations. He made measurements of the accuracy of distance appreciation in vision and in optical illusions. Reaction-time experiments, studies of the time required for a simple act, were also a favorite topic in the early years of the laboratory. Donders and others had been pioneers in this field, but Wundt and his students developed it widely. Wundt began with a study of the simple reaction and measured the time required for action in response to the various sensory stimuli. Then he added various complications, such as action after cognition, or actual appreciation of the stimuli, then discrimination, and finally choice. He was interested in these measurements mainly as furnishing an occasion for the observation and analysis of the processes that preceded action, rather than for their objective results.

After studying the reaction processes for themselves, he used them for studying the association of ideas, and measured the times required for different forms of association. This again was primarily for the study of the order of the associations, and for the discrimination of the different types. Not far removed from this field was the work on the attention processes, especially the range of attention, that was carried out in Wundt's laboratory by Cattell, among the first. Wundt also made much of the so-called complication experiment, in which he studied the influence of attention in bringing sensation to consciousness.

These are but a few of the many investigations conducted in Wundt's laboratory at Leipzig. They serve as samples of the contents of the twenty volumes of the *Philosophische Studien*, which appeared before 1903, most of the contents of which were supplied by workers in that institution. By the time the Leipzig laboratory was thoroughly established, the impulse to do independent experimental work was beginning to spread to other universities, and psychology became a matter not so much of personal systems as of consistent attack by an investigator upon a problem that could be solved by collecting and correlating facts. Systems still existed as they do today, but they were subordinated to the development of methods and to industrious work of experimentation. For this change Wundt was in large degree responsible.

CHAPTER XI

LATER ENGLISH PSYCHOLOGY: SPENCER, BAIN, DARWIN, GALTON

THE two Mills may together be regarded as the founders of English psychology as distinguished from philosophy. Their psychology was a direct outgrowth of philosophy of their earlier countrymen, in so far as it was interested only in determining the laws of succession of mental processes. Spencer and Bain continued this tendency, but they also showed an interest in the physiological substratum of the mental processes, which the Mills had both entirely neglected. There was also added to the doctrines of the earlier English school an attempt to explain the present from the past, the developed human mind from the animal—in short the evolutionary interpretation of mental processes which we first clearly see in Spencer and which was given definite factual support by Darwin. Darwin may be said to have established this evolutionary interpretation so completely that no later psychology was without a trend in this direction.

SPENCER

Herbert Spencer, the son of a schoolmaster, was born at Derby in 1820. He had little systematic schooling in

his earliest years, but picked up a considerable knowledge of natural history for himself. Later he was sent to
an uncle near London who taught him something of the
usual subjects. At seventeen he was apprenticed to a
surveyor and for eight years was employed in engineer-
ing. Then he lost his position and turned to writing,
managing to gain a living by it for the rest of his life,
save for a brief period when he returned to his original calling. After turning to literary work, he lived in
London until 1898, when he moved to Brighton, where
he died in 1903. He became a sub-editor on the *Econ-
omist* in 1846, and published his first book in philosophy, *Social Statics*, in 1850. His most important psychological work, *The Principles of Psychology*, appeared in 1855. In 1860 he proposed to publish by
subscription a series of volumes to constitute his *Synthetic Philosophy;* and the subscriptions received in advance served as a constant spur to keep to his plan of
publication. The entire series of ten volumes was finally
brought to completion, and constitutes one of the most
complete coördinated systems of philosophy in existence, although opinions vary as to its permanent value.

Spencer's *leit motiv* was the notion of development.
Everything must come from something simpler. In this
presentation he was guided by the cosmic theory of La
Place and by Lyell's work in geology. The notion of
evolution was in the air in varying forms, although no

one had fully worked out the details or the mechanism.
Spencer dealt rather in phrases and general principles
than in details or in mechanisms. In a famous phrase
he describes evolution as "a change from incoherent, indefinite homogeneity, to coherent, definite heterogene-
ity." Within the organic series, life is defined as: "the
continuous adjustment of internal relations to external
relations." Consciousness is the accompaniment of the
increasing correspondence and the better adjustment.
The simplest organism shows no difference in its parts,
its activity is a simple shock, and the corresponding consciousness is undifferentiated. With increase in complexity of structure goes increasing variety in consciousness,
as well as greater adaptability to the environment. The
simple reflex as it becomes more complex develops into
the instincts and these develop into definitely volitional
movements.

In his detailed psychology Spencer followed closely
the scheme of the Mills. The elements are simple feelings, which include both sensations and the pleasure-
pain processes. They are compounded by association and
their recall is determined by association. After the more
complex states are formed, they too combine by association and are recalled as wholes. Emotion and will are
closely related to the cognitive elements. Pleasure and
pain are immediate, as was said, and feeling always
tends to arouse movements. Pleasure gives rise to move-

ments of approach, pain to movements of withdrawal. Emotions are compounds of sensations, feelings, and the movements that result from them. Spencer contributed little to the details of psychology for his interest lay mainly in the generalizations. These had a considerable effect upon later writers, and upon his own generation in familiarizing it with the notion of evolution and with a scientific attitude towards psychology.

One important advance he made consisted in giving greater space than was usual in the English school to the physiological mechanism. In the first edition he devotes a relatively short discussion to the physical mechanism of mind somewhat late in the book. In the second edition, published in 1870-1872, he greatly expanded this part, evidently under the influence of Bain, whose *Senses and Intellect* appeared in the same year with Spencer's first edition. In the first edition he gave little concerning physiological structure, although the instincts and reflex were treated as functions of the nervous system. Spencer's notion of the relation between mind and body is interesting as a survival of Spinoza. He thought the two kept step but did not interact. He regarded each as a different manifestation of a common substratum, which he labeled the Unknowable—capitalized to show how important it was even if one could never know more of it than these two expressions, as matter and as consciousness.

BAIN

Alexander Bain, who was more of a psychologist, although possibly less original than Spencer, may be regarded as the final representative of a distinctively English psychology. Even in Bain the influence of Johannes Müller and the other German physiologists began to be apparent, although it is not until the next generation that psychology bears the indication of cosmopolitan science. Bain was born the son of a weaver at Aberdeen in 1818. His education was very irregular. Through poverty, he was compelled to leave school at thirteen and he completed his preparation for college in night school and by himself. He entered Marischall College and received a degree in 1840. For a few years he was assistant in philosophy in the college, then turned to literary work, which he continued until he was elected in 1860 to the chair of logic and English in the University of Aberdeen, newly formed by a combination of Marischall College and King's College. Bain was thus one of the few British psychologists who held a university chair, and even he was a Scot and held the chair in a Scottish university. Bain, as we have said, published *The Senses and The Intellect* in 1855, the same year as Spencer's *Principles*, and in 1859 appeared his *Emotions and the Will*. It was on the basis of these books that he received his appointment. He was active in writing during his period of teaching, bringing out works in rhetoric and logic as well as more general treatises. He perhaps did as much for the science of psychology by starting the publication of the journal *Mind* in 1876 as in any other way, for this made possible the appearance of many psychological articles. Bain retired from his professorship in 1880 on account of ill health but continued writing actively until his death in 1903.

Bain's great contribution to psychology was his organization and systematization of facts which before his time had been scattered among the different sciences, and all of which he brought to bear upon the explanation of mental life. He knew the German physiologists and draws much from Müller in particular; he was interested in the work of the physicists, especially in Wheatstone's work on the stereoscope and related phenomena, and was able to see their bearings upon the problems of mind. In his first book he begins with a complete review of the knowledge developed up to that time of the nervous system, both as structure and as function. Then he devotes a chapter to the muscular sense, in which he dwells not merely upon the awareness it gives of the contraction of those tissues, but also upon the knowledge of spontaneous movement and tonicity that color the entire consciousness. He passes from this to a discussion of the ordinary five senses. He gives particular attention, too, to the sensations from the alimentary canal and other internal organs, being one of the first to be struck by their importance.

In the discussion of the intellectual processes, he follows closely the school of the Mills. He makes much of habit and writes a chapter that almost equals James in vivacity. He lays much more stress upon the active selective processes than did the Mills. On the other hand, he is quite as vigorous in denying any intention of explaining mind as a collection of faculties, a conclusion which is natural if the activity of mental operations is emphasized. The explanation of perception was aided by an appreciation of the influence of movements in the process.

In his second work, *The Emotions and the Will*, Bain continues the same exhaustive eclectic treatment that had marked the first. He develops in considerable detail the notion of instinct, which was much less generally employed before his time. Action depends, in the last analysis, upon the tendency to spontaneous movement which is present in all animals. This is coupled with the tendency for a movement to spread from the muscle group in which it first appears to related and neighboring groups. Emotion is regarded as predominantly motor in character. A group of movements is peculiar to each type of emotion. In this he carried farther the tendency to regard the motor concomitants as a large part of emotion which we have traced from Plato down. He had the advantage in his treatment of the increased knowledge of physiology of his age. His classification of emotions has no definite guiding principle and so contributed little.

Will develops from the same primary factors as emotion. Bain anticipates the notion of "trial and error" introduced forty years later by Thorndike, and makes definite use of the term. He asserts that man has in the beginning a tendency to make spontaneous movements, which are initiated by stimuli but whose course is at first largely due to chance. From these unguided movements those are selected which prove suitable to the organism. Bain also analyses the apparently imitative movements of the child into a similar selection of those movements originating by chance which please the child. He mentions specifically that learning to speak follows this course. When a movement has been repeated a number of times by chance in response to a stimulus, it may then be controlled voluntarily. When the idea appears that has been connected with a movement, the action follows. The idea is the occasion for the movement, but all the energy involved arises from the body. The feeling of effort is usually interpreted as arising from straining muscles, although occasionally he speaks as if it were a sign of the release of physical energy. Bain also might be said to anticipate pragmatism in his statement that action is the test, if not the determining cause, of belief. We believe that upon which we are willing to act.

Bain's general contributions to psychology are difficult to estimate from their very variety and richness. He had the virtues and the vices of an eclectic. Among his virtues may be counted the fact that he brought together for the first time the materials, or most of them, that are now generally accepted as constituting the science of psychology. Thus he prepared the framework that was later to be built upon. Spencer, in a review of the first edition of the *Emotions and the Will,* said that Bain had collected the materials for a psychology but had not written it. Nevertheless Spencer largely rewrote the second edition of his own *Principles of Psychology* on the model that Bain had set. Even if we grant that there is some lack of order, considerable repetition, and a certain amount of inconsistency in it, Bain's work was very valuable. He is full of shrewd observations in detail, and in mass covered the field as no one had done before him. For fifty years he was an accepted authority and he can be read with profit even today.

DARWIN

As has been said, the greatest contribution of the mid-nineteenth century English psychologists was the firm establishment of the principle of evolution. Before this time there had been many developmental theories of mind, but they were usually general in form. After it, all psychology assumed that there had been a development from lower forms of the mental as well as of the physical.

The man who gave the final incentive to the acceptance of this point of view was Charles Darwin.

Charles Darwin was the grandson of Erasmus Darwin (1731–1802), a physician and naturalist who had also made contributions to psychology. He was born at Shrewsbury in 1809, the son of a physician. He began the study of medicine with his father and at the University of Edinburgh, but formed a violent dislike for the practice and turned to theology. To prepare himself for this profession he went to Cambridge. During his residence there he made friendships with many of the men who were working in the natural sciences and became interested in collecting. On graduation he was asked to act as biologist to an expedition which was setting forth in the ship *Beagle* to map the coast of South America. The voyage lasted from 1831 to 1836. On his return he devoted himself to working up the materials collected during the voyage and thus came to devote his life to scientific work. In the main he was entirely without academic or other official connections and so continues the dominant English tradition of a scholar of the amateur type—using the term in its best sense. He died at Down in 1882.

Darwin's main contribution to biological theory came in 1859. He had long been concerned with seeking an explanation of the problem of the varieties of species. Then he chanced to read Malthus's *Essay on Population,* in which the notion is put forth that the population of the earth would, if the birth rate should continue to increase as it was doing at the time of Malthus's writing, soon overtake the possibilities of supplying food, and the weaker must of necessity die off. This suggested to Darwin his notion of the survival of the fittest as the agent in evolution. He worked for twenty years collecting data and weighing the evidence and about convinced himself that his suggestion had been correct. In 1859 A. R. Wallace, who was also a naturalist, read Malthus and was affected much as Darwin had been. He sat down at once and wrote a sketch of a similar evolutionary theory and sent it to Darwin, asking if he thought it tenable and suggesting that he would like to present it at a meeting of the Linnean Society. In the light of his own unpublished results, this put Darwin in a quandary. He referred Wallace's article and a summary of his own results to Sir Charles Lyell, the President of the Linnean Society, with a statement of the circumstances, and asked his advice. Lyell suggested that the two be presented together at the next meeting of the society. And thus the doctrine of the survival of the fit as a method of evolution saw the light. It promptly caused a storm, but the doctrine as a whole was gradually accepted, and it has since dominated all of the biological sciences.

The most important influence of Darwin's work upon psychology lay in its presentation, or rather in its confirmation, of the evolutionary theory. Spencer's statements had been too vague or too general to carry popular opinion. It needed the great accumulation of data that Darwin had gathered and the weight of scientific esteem Darwin enjoyed to carry psychology as a whole into the evolutionist camp. While before Darwin, Spencer alone had taken the evolutionary attitude, after Darwin all psychology was written with the acceptance, explicit or tacit, of the notion of evolution.

Darwin also made specific contributions to psychology. In the *Descent of Man* he shows that many of man's mental capacities can be traced from more rudimentary animal prototypes. He included in these especially those mental and intellectual characteristics which he described as highly important for survival, and in the famous fourth chapter showed that the moral faculties could in certain cases be traced to rudimentary traits in some of the higher animals.

More important was his work on emotional expression. In his *Expression of the Emotions in Man and Animals*, he shows that man's emotional expressions are survivals of movements that were once useful to the animal series. They are now aroused in circumstances that are similar to those in which they were valuable to the animal. Thus while man no longer fights with his teeth, his sneer is a movement similar to that made by a dog when he bares his teeth preparatory to a conflict. He extends this general principle by showing that the expressions may be extended in three ways to related situations. First, the movements are evoked by situations similar to the situation that called forth the full movements by the animal. Second, the movement that is directly opposed in character to the original appears when a situation, the reverse of that which evoked it, is presented to man. Third, certain emotional expressions are to be regarded as mere overflows of nervous energy over any path that may chance to be open. These principles of Darwin are still frequently quoted.

Darwin also made the first concrete study of the activities of a newborn child. This served as a model in method for a number of later works and is still referred to. It was published in 1877 in *Mind*, which had been founded the year before by Bain. Darwin may readily be classed as one of the important English psychologists, even if his main work was done in a different field.

GALTON

Another of the many Englishmen not connected with any institution of learning, who have made important contributions to psychology, was Francis Galton. Galton was also a grandson of Erasmus Darwin and so a cousin of Charles. He was born in 1822, the son of a Birmingham banker. He planned to study medicine but, after a year at King's College, London, and several years at Cambridge, his health failed and he was forced to leave without obtaining a degree. He spent a number of years exploring in Africa and through his contact with the natives became interested in anthropology and consequently in psychology. He was also interested in meteorology, and was Secretary of the British Association for the Advancement of Science from 1863 to 1867. In 1884 he established an anthropometric laboratory at the University of Cambridge, where much excellent work was done. Among the results may be mentioned the development of the process of obtaining and comparing finger prints, now so universally used in identifying criminals. At his death in 1911, Galton left a large sum to found a chair of eugenics in the University of London.

Galton contributed much to psychology in several different fields. His first book that comes within the science was *Hereditary Genius*, published in 1869, in which it is shown that distinguished men are much more likely to have distinguished sons than average individuals are. It was a pioneer work in method and has spurred many to attack the same problem. His *Inquiries on Human Faculty* was of a different character, bringing together a number of psychological studies on varying topics. Two of these—a study of mental imagery and a study of the course of associations—had a lasting influence on the more introspective psychology. In the first he gives an account of his experiments to determine the types of imagery used in recall by men of different occupations and ages. It was here that the classification of imagery into visual, auditory, and motor was introduced, which, together with Galton's method, has been a permanent addition to the science. In connection with association, he showed the regularity of habits of recall in any one person, and the predominance of ideas from relatively early periods of life.

In addition, this volume of studies gave the results of several sensory tests and directions for the performing of these tests, including the preparation and use of series of weights for lifting as a measure of tactile discrimination, and methods for testing the highest audible tone by means of whistles. It also included studies in instincts, in which the gregarious tendencies of animals and man are given especial attention. More in line with Galton's interest in heredity was a study of the characteristics of twins and an interpretation of their similarities and differences in terms of nurture and nature.

Probably Galton's most lasting influence upon psychology came from the part he played in developing a statistical study of human traits, which has influenced the entire testing program of recent times. It was with his aid and encouragement that Karl Pearson began his work on statistical method which led to the development of the methods of determining the coefficients of correlation, now so much used. Although Galton's interests were very varied and he might be called an explorer, a geographer, a meteorologist, and anthropologist, his contributions to psychology make him rank high as a psychologist.

WARD

Still another attitude towards psychology is taken by James Ward, long a professor in Cambridge University, who may be regarded as the first representative in England of the activist school. Ward was born at Hull in 1848. He was educated for the Congregational ministry in Spring Hill College, but after a pastorate of a year at Cambridge became doubtful of the creed and turned to the study of philosophy. He studied psychology by himself and at Göttingen and Berlin, as psychology was not taught at Cambridge in his day. He received the A.M. from Trinity College, was made a fellow in 1875, and University Professor of Philosophy in 1887. He continued at Cambridge until his death in 1925. His most important contribution to psychology was the article "Psychology" in the ninth edition of the Encyclopedia Britannica, published in 1886 and also revised and published separately as the *Principles of Psychology* in 1919.

Ward was definitely hostile to the association type of psychology, and to all psychology that does not include a definite mind. He believed that consciousness, while the immediately given, was not a mere succession of mental states, but was the expression of a controlling central Ego, which gave unity to the whole. Things are represented in mind by presentations, a term that includes sensations, memories, and concepts or objects of thought.

These are reacted to by the Ego or subject in what we call attention. This reaction induces feeling and the character of the feeling depends upon the nature of the reaction in attention. When attention to an object is easy and adequate, pleasure results; when difficulties arise in attending, we have pain or unpleasantness. Feeling, when established, becomes the guide to action. We continue movements that give rise to pleasure, and stop immediately all those that produce pain or discomfort. Conation or the Ego dominates all the changes in consciousness, although older connections are also important. Ward's concrete descriptions are not so different from the writings of Bain, but everything must be reduced to parts of the continuous and self-active whole of consciousness. Mind is more than an aggregation of interacting discrete elements.

STOUT AND SULLY

George F. Stout, born at South Shields in 1860, and since 1903 Professor in the University of St. Andrews, follows Ward in making consciousness primarily conative in character. Every experience has an intellectual, an effective, and a conative aspect, but the conative is the most important and the others are to be derived from it. He makes introspection the primary psychological method and regards experiment as contributing nothing significant, although he did make much use of experimental results in his books. He is important rather for the clearness of his statements and the comprehensive treatment that he gives of psychology, than for his own contributions. James Sully may also be mentioned in the same way. He was for long professor of psychology in University College, London, and wrote *The Human Mind* and other shorter works. These reveal his wide acquaintance with the subject and his conservative attitude, but add little in theory or in fact to psychology.

RIVERS, MYERS, McDOUGALL

The next generation of English psychology was dominated by a group of Cambridge men who chanced to go together on the Cambridge University Torres Strait expedition in 1898–99. They were selected to make anthropological and psychological tests upon the natives and brought back the results of numerous sensory tests as well as much more general material. The group consisted of W. H. R. Rivers, C. S. Myers, and William McDougall. Rivers (1864–1922) was connected with St. Johns College, Cambridge, in various ranks until he became its head. He published numerous works bearing upon anthropology and psychology, and worked with Head in a study of the effects upon tactual sensation of the regeneration of a peripheral nerve. During the war all three of these men were in the medical service and Rivers published numerous articles and several books based on experiences with victims of shock and related phenomena. In the main he is critical of the extreme claims of the Freudian school.

Myers (1873–   ) was in charge of the psychological laboratory at Cambridge and later became head of an Institute of Industrial Psychology in London for the application of psychological methods and results to business and industry. He worked with special problems of sound localization and covered the field fairly well. With Ward in 1904 he founded the *British Journal of Psychology*, which continues to be the main vehicle for publication of British work in psychology.

McDougall (1871–   ) was reader in psychology at Oxford and directed the laboratory there until 1919, when he came to Harvard. His system will be considered in Chapter XVIII.

CHAPTER XII

LATER GERMAN PSYCHOLOGY: BRENTANO, G. E. MÜLLER, EBBINGHAUS, STUMPF, LIPPS, KÜLPE

WHILE Wundt dominated German psychology for a few years after the founding of the Leipzig laboratory, he was not unchallenged for long. Müller at Göttingen, Stumpf at Berlin, and, even earlier, Brentano at Würzburg and Vienna, began movements that developed under different traditions, and inclined to question the spirit and especially the general principles on which Wundt had built. Possibly nowhere in the world are academic rivalries so intense as in Germany, and they were especially bitter in psychology. Wundt also had students who set up laboratories in other universities and continued his teachings and methods with various modifications. It was not long before many contending schools had developed. They differed from the earlier schools in that they all recognized and used the experimental method and made actual contributions of fact, however they might differ in interpretation.

BRENTANO

Brentano belongs among the contemporaries rather than the successors of Wundt. He was about Wundt's age, but he developed his work from different principles and arrived at different conclusions. He was born at Marienburg in 1838. A student in philosophy and theology in Munich and Tübingen, he entered the priesthood in 1864 and the same year became *docent* in philosophy at Würzburg. Here his lectures in philosophy attracted more than ordinary attention. Among his students there was Stumpf; also Meinong, who founded the first psychological laboratory in Austria, at Graz, in 1894. When in 1870 the decree establishing the doctrine of papal infallibility was promulgated, Brentano felt that he would soon be compelled to sever his relations with the church. His scepticism concerning many church doctrines grew until, in 1872, he was convinced that he could no longer honestly retain his priestly office and withdrew from orders. Meantime he had been advanced to full professor, but when he left the priesthood he also resigned from the university. In 1874 he was called to Vienna to the full professorship of philosophy and taught there until 1880 when he resigned his chair and devoted the remainder of his life to private study and occasional writing. He had his home near Vienna until 1895. He then settled in Florence to remain until 1917 when, on account of the war, he went to Switzerland where he died in the same year. He was always surrounded by a wide circle of friends and admirers, exercising a greater influence through them than by his writings.

Although Brentano wrote his main work, *Psychologie vom empirischen Standpunkt*, in 1874, he was relatively late in being widely recognized, at least there was a wide renewal of recognition just before and just after his death. This was partly because of the fragmentary character of his writings. His *Psychologie* was published as the first volume of a larger work, the remainder of which however was never completed. After his death Kraus collected a few notes of his lectures preserved by students, but these give the only indication of what their projected continuation would have been. Brentano approached psychology from the standpoint of Aristotle, whose works he studied profoundly. He was convinced that the wide diversity of opinion in psychology could be avoided by a suitable approach and that there should be *a* psychology instead of psychologies, as there have been through the course of history. He believed this could be accomplished by making psychology rigidly empirical, although not necessarily experimental after the manner of Wundt. He asserted that it was useless to attempt to deduce a psychology from the nature of the soul. On the contrary, one can directly observe the mental processes and these alone should be the objects of psychological study. They should be studied by direct observation. He also insisted that mental phenomena, not mind, should be regarded as the data of psychology.

Mental processes were acts rather than passive processes, and were to be regarded as acts of mind. As experiences they were different from all other events in that they always had reference to something beyond themselves. They always meant something and were important for their meaning rather than for themselves. In his classification of mental processes, Brentano went back to Aristotle in combining action and emotion into a single group, which he called the love-hate group. All action and all emotion are derived from one or the other of these two processes. The mere experiences are designated ideas, whether they come directly from sense or are revived. He differed from all others in making fundamental the distinction between having an idea and judging it to be true or false. The three forms of mental phenomena, then, are ideas, judgments, and emotion or appetition. It would be truer to say that Brentano's fundamental forms of mental phenomena are awareness, judging, and reacting emotionally or actively, since he regards every bit of experience as an act, not a state.

He did not work out the details of his system any farther. He spends several pages in justifying his classification and in developing a proof of the unity of consciousness, but applications are incidental only. In spite of its fragmentary character, Brentano's *Psychologie* had a profound influence on general principles, although rather by way of contrasting background than through its general acceptance. It influenced the theories of the philosophers, especially of the Husserl school, and of the logicians, including Meinong, Höfler, and Marty.

EBBINGHAUS

The number of men who developed psychology on the experimental side was very great, and we can mention only a few of them. Of the older group, born near the middle of the last century, we may pass five in rapid review. One of the first men to make advances in a field little worked by Wundt was Hermann Ebbinghaus. Ebbinghaus was born at Barmen in 1850, was made assistant professor at Berlin in 1886, was called to the full chair at Breslau in 1894, was transferred to Halle in 1905 and died there in 1909. He was a pioneer in detailed experiments with memory, and invented several of the methods that have since become standard. He chose as the material to be learned in his memory experiments nonsense syllables made by combining two consonants with a vowel between. He made as many such combinations as possible and then eliminated all that made sense. These were printed on separate cards and the cards were so shuffled that each was exposed to view for two-fifths of a second. Ebbinghaus made all his experiments upon himself. He would repeat a series of twelve or sixteen cards until he could say them once through without mistake and then would determine how many repetitions were necessary to relearn after a given time. The difference measured the amount of forgetting. By this method he established the law that forgetting goes on rapidly at first and then more and more slowly. More definitely he found that forgetting is a function of the logarithm of the time involved.

Among the more important laws which he established is the law that learning is a direct function of the number of repetitions. He tested the number of repetitions up to sixty-four when the number required for perfect learning was thirty. This means that overlearning, within limits, shows in the delayed recall. He also proved that there is a marked increase in the number of repetitions required if the number of syllables in a series is increased. He also demonstrated the law that associative connections are formed not only between contiguous syllables but also between syllables separated by from one to eight others. He also showed that associations are formed in a backward as well as in a forward direction. The work itself was a model of patient application, and the results and methods opened a new chapter in psychology. His general treatise on psychology, *Die Grundzüge der Psychologie*, was one of the clearest formulations of facts and principles of its time and contributed much in new analyses on important problems. It was first published in 1902.

G. E. MÜLLER

An important man whose life spans the period from before Lotze's death to the present is Georg Elias Müller. He was born at Grimma in 1850, studied at the universities of Berlin, at Leipzig, and finally at Göttingen under Lotze. He began his university career as a *docent* at Göttingen in 1876 and succeeded Lotze in the professorship in 1881. He began experimental work while still an assistant and before Wundt's laboratory was founded. He has sometimes intimated that he might claim the honor of initiating experimental psychology. He was certainly one of the very early men to begin laboratory work. He retired from his professorship in 1922, continuing to live and work at Göttingen. Müller's reputation rests upon a series of monographs on very different topics rather than upon any one systematic work or body of principles.

Müller's first important monograph was a theory of sensory attention, published in 1873. In this he gives a thoroughly objective analysis of the attention process in which he finds the causal force in preceding ideas, in the circulatory processes, and in the interaction of the active portions of the cerebrum. He eliminates the notion of a separate force or faculty of attention. A second monograph which attracted still more readers was the *Fundamental Facts of Psychophysics (Grundtatsachen der Psychophysik)*, published in 1878, a criticism of Fechner's conclusions concerning Weber's Law. In this he argues for a physiological rather than a psychophysical interpretation of the law. Weber's Law, it will be remembered, states that the amount which must be added to any stimulus to make a just noticeable difference is a constant fraction of that stimulus. When the stimulus is faint, a relatively slight absolute addition will be noticed; when the stimulus is intense, a much greater addition must be made before it can be appreciated. Fechner explained the need for a stronger added stimulus when the original stimulus was great on the assumption that there was always something lost when the excitation passed from body to mind, and that the loss was always in the same ratio, after the analogy of a percentage tariff at the border of a foreign country. Müller used the same analogy, but asserted that the loss was within the nervous system. The slighter stimuli used up the more readily oxidized substances in the nerves and if an added excitation was to be produced when the nerve was already strongly excited, a correspondingly greater stimulus was required. Recent knowledge of nervous action renders the theory antiquated, but it showed a marked tendency to demand specific rather than vague explanations which was rare at the time it was published. Still later Müller contributed a modification of the Hering color theory and extended the discussion of spatial localization.

Müller's great claim to distinction is to be found

in his continuation and extension of Ebbinghaus's work on memory. He added a new method that proved fruitful. The Ebbinghaus method measured only potential memory, the amount of material that might be made effective by new learning. Müller measured the amount of effective memory, the material that could be actually used at the time of measuring. He made his tests on memorizing a series of syllables by learning them in pairs, and then after the lapse of a given time would present the first syllable of a pair and ask the subject to supply the second member. The percentage of right answers measured the retention. He showed his syllables by means of a cylinder that revolved at a regular speed behind a small slot and thus insured presentation at regular intervals. He also connected his apparatus with an electrically controlled clock, in such a way that the clock started when the syllable was shown and ran until the second syllable was spoken, thus measuring the time required for recall.

A large number of the more important laws of memory were discovered by Müller and his students. They found that one can learn much more easily and quickly by reading each selection to be memorized through from beginning to end, than by learning it bit by bit and putting the parts together as one usually does. Also they demonstrated the so-called law of divided repetitions, to the effect that one learns with fewer repetitions if one permits a day or more to intervene between successive readings.

We may also mention the numerous types of inhibition or interference between associative connections which Müller developed. He found that if one syllable had been associated with a given syllable, and then an attempt was made to connect a second syllable with the given one, much more time was required than would have been necessary if the first syllable had not been already learned in association with the original one. He showed that the two associates thus made with the same first syllable also interfered with each other at the time of recall. One was less likely to recall either, and the recalling took a longer time, than if one association alone had been formed. He also proved that partially set associations are disturbed by trying to learn something else or to do any severe mental work immediately after the first has been learned. His work with Dr. Rückle, a memory prodigy, was also striking and served to establish many laws of normal memory. He used these experiments as the basis for three volumes on memory in all of its manifestations, published as monograph supplements to the *Zeitschrift für Psychologie* in 1911 and 1913.

STUMPF

Karl Stumpf, long director of the psychological laboratory at the University of Berlin, was also a pupil of Lotze, studying with Brentano as well. Stumpf was born in Wiesenfeld, Franken, in 1848. He was a student at Würzburg and later at Göttingen. He became *docent* at Würzburg and in the course of his advancement held chairs at Prag, Halle, and Munich. He was called to Berlin in 1894 and continued there until his retirement in 1921. Even after his official retirement he continued his courses, on occasion. Like Müller, Stumpf published his results in separate monographs and has not written a comprehensive systematic work. Among his important works is his book on the origin of the *Idea of Space* (*Ursprung der Raumvorstellung*), published in 1873. In this he takes a nativistic attitude towards the problem of space, believing that in its essentials at least it is complete before experience. He challenged Helmholtz's empirical theory of musical consonance also, in his *Psychology of Tone* (*Tonpsychologie*), one volume of which was published in 1883, the other in 1890. He asserts that one is immediately aware of both a feeling of pleasure and a unity in the octave and of duplicity and dissonance in two notes a half tone apart that cannot be due to beats or other extraneous factors. His latest work (*Die Sprachlaute*) on the quality of vowel sounds, begun when he was seventy years old and published in 1926, is a tribute to his persistence and to his mental health in old age. He compounded the vowels from elementary tones and thus determined the nature of the different vowels. Stumpf continued the German tradition of working in philosophy as well as in psychology. His is a strong personality that stimulated many men to careful work in experiment and to fruitful thought in the more theoretical problems.

LIPPS

Theodor Lipps, who also belongs in this period, is known for his theoretical rather than his experimental contributions. Born in Waülallen, in the Rhenish palatinate, in 1851 he was successively professor at Bonn and Breslau, and then at Munich until his death in 1913. Lipps shows the influence of Herbart, of Wundt, and of Brentano, although not directly a disciple of any one of them. With all of them he restricts the data of psychology to the mental processes but like Brentano he regards the mental processes as the result of an activity of the central self upon the after-effect of some earlier activity. We are aware, however, of the results of the interaction alone, and not at all of the primary self. Like Wundt, he makes much use of the term apperception to indicate activity. His psychology is highly abstract and makes little attempt to connect the products of his thinking with the events of daily life. This in spite of the fact that he made experiments and directed the work of students in the investigation of space and time.

The contribution that attracted most attention was Lipps's introduction of the notion of *Einfühlung*. This arose through his belief that one can know directly only the self and its reactions. He divided knowledge into three types: knowledge of things, knowledge of one's own self, and knowledge of other selves. Both things and other selves, however, can be known only in so far as we read our own selves into them, really feel ourselves into them. He introduces his discussion of *Einfühlung* in these terms and then proceeds to show how we put ourselves in the place of all the objects that we really perceive. In looking at lines we appreciate them only as we put ourselves in their place. Thus he explains the fact that vertical lines seem longer than horizontal lines. The vertical line suggests ourselves standing, while a horizontal line suggests ourselves lying down. The former requires more effort and so seems longer. Similarly a column too small for the load it is carrying is ugly because we think of the effort that would be called for were we in its place. All aesthetic enjoyment is explained in this way, as the result of a projection of the observer into it. Lipps published this theory in its full form in his two volume *Aesthetik* in 1906.

KÜLPE

To the next generation belongs Oswald Külpe, a pupil of Wundt, who showed much originality. He was born in Candau, Courland, in 1862. He received his degree from Leipzig and then became *docent* and assistant in

the Institute of Psychology. Later he was professor in Würzburg, Bonn, and at Munich where he died in 1915. Probably his most characteristic work was done while he was at Würzburg, which has led to frequent references to his work as being of the Würzburg School. Külpe's great charm of manner and friendly attitude towards his students, foreign as well as native, together with his great ability, attracted many to his classes.

He is known for his work on centrally aroused sensations, which studied experimentally the differences that mark off memory-images from the direct external or peripherally aroused sensations. He used the term to indicate at once the close similarity between memories and the immediate sensations from the objects they represent, and the differences in origin of the two processes. Possibly the most important work of his school was that which bore upon thought. An earlier group had emphasized the great influence of a set task or mental attitude upon attention and thinking. Külpe himself observed the effect of the task upon the observation of objects, and showed that one sees in a situation what corresponds to the task in mind as one looks. Watt showed that associations were controlled by the same factor. He would show a word asking the subject to name the class to which it belonged, and found that the word for the class would appear at once; if the task set was to give an instance of the class to which the word belonged, that would come just as certainly. This result was confirmed and extended by Ach and numerous others.

Most closely connected with the Würzburg School is the notion of imageless thought, the belief that it is possible to represent meanings without having any specific mental imagery. Watt, Messer, Bühler and others of the school reported many instances of controlled introspection in which they knew that they were thinking of a definite problem or had reached a conclusion without having any specific mental content present. The report of the experiments brought out a vigorous protest from Wundt, and was warmly supported or as bitterly opposed by many others in various countries. The observations and their explanation is still a matter of discussion in many places.

This group of workers may be regarded as intermediate between the great systematizers of the pre-Wundtian period and the emergence of new distinct schools. They made it a period when there was coöperation in collecting experimental data, even if there were marked differences of opinion.

KRAEPELIN AND MEUMANN

To this group we may add the names of Kraepelin and Meumann. Kraepelin was the greatest of the German psychiatrists of the last generation, and also did several bits of work with a psychological bearing. He was born at Neustrelitz in 1856, studied with Wundt at Leipzig, became Professor of Psychiatry at Dorpat, Heidelberg and Munich successively, and died in 1927. In psychiatry he completely revised the classification of mental diseases, making a relatively few general classes where there had been numerous badly defined groups before. This classification was generally accepted in all countries. Since the Freudian movement, the theory behind the classification has been changed and alternative names suggested for two diseases, but the groups and clinical pictures are retained. Kraepelin also did much excellent work on specifically psychological problems. We owe to him the generally accepted analysis of the fatigue processes.

Ernst Meumann (1862–1915), Professor at Zurich and later at Königsberg, Halle, and Hamburg, may also be mentioned for his investigations on memory. They were among the more notable bits of work in that field.

CHAPTER XIII

FRENCH PSYCHOLOGY OF THE NINETEENTH CENTURY AND AFTER

FRENCH psychology at the end of the eighteenth century and the beginning of the nineteenth was closely interwoven with philosophy—a philosophy, however, of an empirical type that did not go much beyond a psychology of sensation and ideas. During the revolution the principles of Condillac [1] dominated the field. These gradually received modification through the interest in abnormal mental states which has given a distinctive touch to French psychology down to the present. Later the Scotch School became influential.

DE TRACY AND CABANIS

The ideologues, among whom we may name Destut de Tracy and Cabanis, were the most faithful of the disciples of Condillac, although each made advances upon him. Tracy insisted that awareness of our own movements through sensations from the muscles were necessary to give a real idea of external objects. It is only when the moving member meets resistance that we can be sure a sensation comes from without. Cabanis related the sensations to the brain in giving a material-

[1] See Page 101.

istic touch to sensationalism. Only the impressions came from without and these were transformed into sensations in the brain, much as food was changed into nourishment in the stomach.

DE BIRAN AND LAROMIGUIERE

After the ideologues came a reaction to voluntarism. Maine de Biran insisted that the real knowledge of anything arose from the active response we make to it and is not a mere sum of sensations. This reaction may come from the movement of the body, or it may be the direct result of attending to the sensation which is itself a voluntary act. Laromiguière extended the doctrine. For the "I think, therefore I am" of Descartes, these men would substitute: "I will, therefore I am." Attention controls ideas and ideas in turn direct action. Knowledge is more fundamental, but action as choice was the final determinant of the world and of man in it. They introduced the common sense justification of the existence of the external world. In this they passed from mere sensations to the objects outside.

COMTE

Comte should also be mentioned in our history, for in spite of the fact that he did not believe a psychology possible, he had considerable influence in developing one. As a positivist, he would gather facts and let them speak for themselves with as little interpretation and theory as possible. This ideal tended to favor the collection of specific observations, and to develop an experimental rather than a merely rational treatment of all sciences, and psychology profited from the attitude. Comte reiterated the statement, which we have met before and seen to be refuted by Tetens, that one could never obtain a knowledge of mental states through observation or introspection, because the fact of observation would of itself change the state. Instead of psychology, curiously enough, he advocated phrenology where the errors were very much more profound. As the founder of sociology, Comte's influence was more direct upon social psychology than upon any other branch.

PINEL

The French early became interested in the light which mental disease might throw upon the nature of normal mental processes. During the French Revolution, Pinel became impressed with the idea that the insane were after all only individuals with diseased brains, and that they offered much material that could be used in understanding the ordinary processes. On the humanitarian side he appreciated that the then current methods of treating the insane, by keeping them in prison and in chains under loathsome conditions, was not only illogical but cruel. He fostered a movement that should substitute hospitals for dungeons, and physicians and nurses for jailers in caring for these unfortunates. He accomplished much on the practical side, and he began the change in theory that gradually led public opinion to see that an insane man was not a man possessed of a devil, and so an outcast in a Christian nation, but merely an unfortunate creature who should be cured rather than punished. Esquirol, with a more definite psychological and philosophical interest, followed Pinel in this approach, and gained much for psychology from his work with the abnormal, and much for his practice from his psychological approach.

TAINE

The last of the purely philosophical French psychologists was Hippolyte Taine, who was born at Vouziers, in the Ardennes, in 1828, entered the École Normale in 1848, and was given his *docteur ès lettres* in 1853. Taine taught for a few years in the provincial *lycées*, but soon felt that for political reasons the authorities were not favorable to him, and resigned to devote himself to writing. Much of his work was in literature, but his *Theory of Intelligence* attracted much attention and was recognized as a standard authority, as is shown by its popularity in the English translation as well as in the original.

Taine's psychology was an associationism, based more on the Mills than on Condillac. He began with an analysis of ideas as symbols and passed thence to a consideration of the nature of abstract ideas and the way in which thought depends upon them. Then he introduced a discussion of concrete images. From that he went back to the conventional discussion of sensations of different types, which were as well treated as the knowledge of the day permitted. A description of the nervous system and its functions followed. The laws of perception and the education of the senses received much space, as did the laws of reasoning and the ways in which we know the physical body. He ended with a discussion of the nature of the self. While the main outline of his theory is derived from the Mills, much more emphasis is placed upon the active and self directive functions than in the English school. Taine also drew largely upon the material drawn from the revived interest in hypnotism and the abnormal mental states that Charcot and his follower were beginning to show. These made his treatment of illusions and of delusions, and of the disturbances of the self, illuminating.

RIBOT

The more specifically psychological work in France begins with Ribot, who did much himself and was the inspiration of much more. Born in 1839 at Guincamp,

Théodulc Armand Ribot entered the École Normale in 1862, received the degree of *agrégé* in 1867, and the *docteur ès lettres* in 1875. He taught in various *lycées* until he became professor at the Sorbonne in 1885, and was then given the professorship of experimental psychology at the Collège de France in 1888. He died in 1919, at Paris. Aside from his writings, he probably did most for psychology by founding and editing the *Revue Philosophique,* beginning in 1875, which always published much psychological material. Ribot's writings consisted of discussions of single topics rather than of comprehensive treatises. He combined the psychology of the English and German schools, which his historical writings show that he knew well, with the work of physicians in mental pathology. Two important publications that draw largely on the pathology of mental life, are the *Diseases of Memory* and the *Diseases of Personality*. *Diseases of Memory* outlines first a general theory that starts with the Hering notion of organic memory, passes to the importance of recognition, and finally gives a summary of the facts concerning the partial and complete destruction of memory. *Diseases of Personality* is one of the first general accounts of dissociation of personality, with a collection of the cases reported up to that time. In it Ribot also considers the deterioration in personality that comes with various types of more profound mental disease. He finds the self best understood as the final coördinated action of the organism as a whole, represented in the cerebral cortex, and expressed in a unified consciousness, to which all experience, past and present, contributes.

Ribot's *Psychology of Attention* contains what is probably his most striking contribution. His thesis here is that attention is closely related to physical action, and that it is the result of anticipatory movement. The movements involved in the adjustment of the sense organs are evident to all, but in addition to these Ribot asserts that the voluntary muscles in all parts of the body and even the muscles controlled by the sympathetic system, the unstriped muscles, are aroused to activity during attention and aid in determining its character. Attention would not take the course that it does without them. Ribot extends the same notion of the dependence of consciousness upon preceding bodily movements to other fields. In this general direction he anticipates the theory of James and Lange, not in the application of the principles to emotion, but in the general notion that one may have a consciousness which derives its really important qualities from the awareness of bodily responses themselves initiated reflexly. He has had a host of followers in applying this general theory in all fields.

In his *Psychology of the Emotions,* published considerably after James's work, Ribot goes a step farther than did James in making the physical responses and the mental accompaniment different phases of the same process and relating them as Aristotelian form to matter.

He also anticipates McDougall in making instinct and emotion different phases of the same fundamental physiological process. In general he sees emotions as the awareness of the vague fundamental drives or appetites which have remained at a low level of evolution and so are accompanied by only vague consciousness. Intellect develops with a complete awareness and understanding of the situation and the processes that result from it.

Ribot's books may stand as evidence of the wide range of interest their author showed. He did much to encourage other workers and was a living force in French psychology for nearly two generations.

BINET

Alfred Binet made many contributions which were more specifically experimental. Binet was born in Nice in 1857, was educated at a Paris *lycée*, and in the law school from which he received his degree in 1878. His real interest, however, was in the biological sciences, and while yet engaged in his law course, he was attracted to the Salpêtrière, where Charcot was at the zenith of his powers. Before he had developed a law practice, he turned to writing. His first two works, *The Psychic Life of Microorganisms* and the *Psychology of Reasoning*, indicate the wide range of his interests. Beaunis had established a laboratory of experimental psychology at the Sorbonne in 1889, and in 1892 Binet was appointed as his assistant. He at once began a vigorous experimental program which continued to his death. When Beaunis retired because of ill health in 1894, Binet succeeded him as chief. In 1895 he brought out the first volume of *L'Année psychologique*, which became at once the most important organ in France for the publication of experimental material and has held that preëminence to the present. A vigorous experimental worker and ingenious theorist, he died an untimely death in 1911.

Binet's first publications were directed by his work with Charcot towards the abnormal. His *Animal Magnetism*, written in collaboration with Féré, represented the attitude of the Salpêtrière school on that subject. The *Alternations of Personality* shows a similar bent. These prepared the way for his later interest in the feeble-minded. Very different in character was his *Psychology of Reasoning*, in which he argued that reasoning is of the same general character as perception, and that both are to be explained by association through similarity. Perception always involves interpretation although we are aware of the result, not of the process. Reasoning is only carrying farther this same fundamental process. A later book, the *Étude expérimentale de L'Intelligence*, develops the theory that much thought is without definite images and that the essential activities of reasoning do not exhibit themselves in images. This work was based upon a long experimental study of the mental life of the author's young daughters, and in its conclusions anticipated the work of the Würzburg school to which we have already referred.

Binet is generally best known for his development of the scale of tests used in measuring intelligence. A commission appointed by the French authorities to devise means for dealing with feebly endowed children, found they could not approach their problem until they had a means for determining who was feeble-minded. They turned to Binet who undertook to discover a means of measuring intelligence. Binet collaborated with Simon in a long series of experiments on the Paris school children to develop a set of tasks in which the normal child would progress regularly with age. When this was found it was possible to apply the same scale to a mentally defective individual of any age and measure his capacity by comparing the tests he could pass with those passed by the normal child. His mental age was the age of the average child who could pass the same tests. This resulted in the famous Binet-Simon scale that has been applied in modified form in most countries.

Binet's last years were devoted to the studies of defectives and to the problems of thought that grew out of them. Many extended monographs, which appeared during these last years, some published separately, many in *L'Année psychologique*, contained the results of special investigations. His early death prevented the completion of a system of psychology which was planned to give a complete presentation of his more general conclusions.

PIÉRON, BOURDON, FOUCAULT

Of the other French psychologists of our day, Piéron may be mentioned as continuing the work of Binet at the laboratory of the Sorbonne, and as editor of *L'Année psychologique*. He has also published numerous monographs on subjects ranging from memory to sleep. Recently he has adopted a modified form of behaviorism as his guiding principle. Bourdon, one of the early students of Wundt, has been active at the University of Rennes, since he returned to France. His work on space perception contains much new material as well as summaries of the work of others, including an especially complete account of the perception of those born blind who have recovered sight. Marcel Foucault has been an equally active experimenter at Montpellier for almost as long a period.

SCHINTZ
BOAS

HAYES
TITCHENER

HOLT
CATTELL

WHIPPLE

DREW

WILSON
SANFORD
BRILL

PORTER

GODDARD
KANDA
BURNHAM

CHAMBERLAIN
JENNINGS

DAWSON
SEASHORE
JAMES

BALDWIN
JASTROW

WELLS
STERN

BUCHNER
BURGERSTEIN
KATZEN
HALL

KIRKPATRICK
ELLENBORGER

FREUD

FERENZI
JONES

KARLSON
JUNG

KAKISE
MEYER

CHAPTER XIV

PSYCHOLOGY IN AMERICA

THE history of psychology in America may be said to begin with the eighties of the last century. Before that there had been occasional men who wrote psychological books, but most of them wrote in the spirit of the theologian or echoed European work, in the main, of the less significant movements. In the colonial period Jonathan Edwards is mentioned for his advocacy of determinism of action, but his was primarily an expression of a Calvinistic theology rather than the result of psychological considerations. Down to 1875 or 1880, the teaching of psychology was largely in the hands of college presidents, who received their appointments for their eloquence in the pulpit and in their administrative ability rather than for any intellectual attainment or scholarship. If they had scholarly interests at all, they were much more likely to be philosophical than psychological.

McCOSH

One of the men who deserve more than passing mention is James McCosh, who came to Princeton from Belfast in 1868 when disappointed in his efforts to receive the appointment at Aberdeen won by Bain. He was for a long time professor of philosophy and President of Princeton University. An adherent in the strictest form of the Scotch School, he wrote volumes on *The Cognitive Powers* and on *The Motive Powers* that had a psychological bearing, but gave no great evidence of originality. Similarly Bowne, Professor of Philosophy at Boston University, was a devoted follower of Lotze and did much to introduce and extend his doctrines in America. Still earlier, Henry Tappan, President of the University of Michigan, did something of an original character in a volume on *The Will* in which he defends free will against the attacks of Edwards. Finally, as the last of the pre-scientific school, may be mentioned President Noah Porter of Yale, who in his *Human Intellect* gave an eclectic treatment of psychology which discusses topics ranging from sensation to the nature of matter, and takes into consideration the theories involved from Aristotle to Lotze.

America's awakening to the importance of psychology came through three different influences: that of James, who had approached the subject from the angle of physiology; that of Wundt's work, which was brought over by Stanley Hall, Cattell, and soon after by many others; and that of Ladd at Yale who had come to a gradual appreciation of what was being done elsewhere. These sources of inspiration seem to have been fairly independent, although a knowledge of developments abroad seems to have had its effect on the men who developed separately in America. Of these James was the most important, certainly the most original, and probably had most followers.

JAMES

William James was born in 1842, the son of a man of great learning who had also a somewhat mystical temperament, shown in his interest in the writings of Swedenborg. The son had a long and varied education with a number of successive aims. He studied French at Geneva and German at Bonn, aside from his American school work. After studying painting for a time, he entered Harvard, where after several shifts he finally received a degree in medicine, which, however, he never practised. After graduation, he spent a year with Agassiz collecting on the Amazon, and then returned to take an instructorship in anatomy at Harvard. Later he transferred to comparative anatomy and physiology. As time went on he came to be especially interested in the physiology of the nervous system and the other phases of physiology related to the mental life. In the late seventies he began experiments in a small way that would now pass for psychological experiments and through them might claim to have established the first psychological laboratory. In 1880 he became officially assistant professor of philosophy, then in 1889, professor of psychology. He took the title of professor of philosophy after Münsterberg came to Harvard in 1897.

James began to write on psychological topics in the eighties, mostly in *Mind,* and was a frequent contributor during that decade. This line of work reached its climax with the publication of his *Principles of Psychology* in 1890. This book contained many of the articles that had been previously published, but also much that was printed for the first time. With the publication of this work James began to lose interest in psychology. Two years later he published a *Briefer Course,* for use as a textbook, which was largely a condensation of the original *Principles,* and this marked the end of his important contributions to psychology proper. Both books had a large sale and the *Briefer Course* was used for a generation by many institutions. He devoted himself to philosophy after this, except for one popular address, *Talks to Teachers on Psychology.* James retired from his chair in 1907 and died in 1910.

The Principles of Psychology won instant recognition because of its style, its vividness of statement, and its fairness of treatment, as well as the originality of many of its theories. It is valuable rather for the brilliancy of its separate parts than for the presentation of a system. In a famous letter to Stumpf, James criticizes Wundt's system, or lack of system, in the words: "Cut him up like a worm and each fragment crawls; there is no *noeud*

vital in his system, so that you can't kill him all at once." The same statement may be applied to James's own presentation. However, it is a question whether, in the tentative stage of development in which psychology then was and probably still is, this characteristic is not an advantage rather than a drawback. James's great virtue was that he attempted to understand mental life as a concrete experience without more dogmas than were absolutely necessary. To do this he found it essential to shift his fundamental presuppositions from time to time, even from chapter to chapter, and not to notice the shift. Each chapter was written as a separate contribution and often it was published before it appeared in the book. What he lost in consistency he gained in directness and perhaps in truth. The book is probably the most interesting work on psychology ever written.

In general plan, James followed very much the order of Bain and Wundt, by beginning with a discussion of the nervous system and its action before going into psychology proper. He deviated from this and from the arrangement usual at present, by postponing the discussion of the sensations to the second volume. James reaped the reward of his long apprenticeship to physiology in his ability to deal at first hand with the facts of neurology. His treatment of the localization of functions gave a summary of the opposing positions that was final for that day. The chapter on the "stream of consciousness" presents with great literary art a criticism of atomism in psychology. He insists that mind is not given in teacups-full or in other arbitrary units, but that all mental processes are but phases of the unitary continuous whole of experience that runs without sharp break from birth to death. He also opposes the notion of the associationist that ideas are definite units conjoined by laws of association. On the contrary, the connections have no real basis save in the interaction of the neural elements. The final result is the association of things, not ideas. The meanings are distinct, but not the mental processes. Ideas are, on the one hand, mere accompaniments of the fundamental neural activities. On the other, they are distinct only because they mean different things.

The most striking of the chapters are those on habit, on the self, on emotion, on will, and on instincts, in which the long series of discussions and enumerations of instincts from Darwin down is given a systematic form. Any one of these could be recommended to the general reader, the interest of the material itself being its own reward. Possibly the theory that is most original, at least that which has been given greatest recognition, is the theory of the emotions as back-strokes from muscular contractions. We have traced the recognition of bodily processes as important for the emotions from Plato down. Many writers had given a fairly definite seat to the different emotions. Most however pictured the emotion as a mental process which comes first and causes some change in the body. In an article published in

Mind in 1884 and reprinted with little change in the *Principles,* James insisted that all of his predecessors had failed to put emotion and bodily response in the right order. Really the bodily process is an immediate reflex response to the stimulus, and the emotion appears only when the individual appreciates these bodily changes. When a man sees a bear he does not run because he is afraid, but he is afraid because he runs. The emotion is merely the consciousness of the visceral and other automatic movements that are aroused at once through physiological connections when the stimulus affects the subject.

In 1887, without having heard of the James theory, Karl Lange, a Dane, published his *Ueber die Gemüths-bewegung,* a volume that expressed almost the same point of view. The theory is usually referred to as the James-Lange theory. This theory has been the subject of bitter controversy from its first statement to the present. It seemed to be meeting fairly general acceptance until 1928, when Cannon, some of whose earlier work seemed to substantiate the theory, came to the opinion that the bodily responses to opposed emotions were too nearly alike to give the profound conscious differences, and suggested that one must seek the quality of the emotion in the response of the lower brain centers, especially in the thalamus. Whether finally accepted or not, the James theory had a profound influence on the psychological thought of a generation.

James's freedom in changing his point of view, even his fundamental premises, appears most clearly in his discussion of the self and the will. In his famous chapter on the self in the first volume of his *Principles*, he begins by discussing the problem without any presuppositions as to a metaphysical self. There are several kinds of self: a bodily self, that is made up of sensations from the body through the internal and external senses; a social self, the man as he thinks other people think of him; the spiritual self, and the pure Ego. The chapter is devoted to a discussion of what one can see in direct experience that can be given a connotation of self, and practically nothing is made of any substantial thing or force behind it all. In his conclusion James says: "If the passing thought be the directly verifiable existent which no school has hitherto doubted it to be, then that thought is itself the thinker, and psychology need not look beyond." He admits the possibility of abandoning psychology for metaphysics and introducing a knower, but inclines to the belief that it is not necessary, and that psychology has no right to deal with such hypotheses. In his last years in reporting to the Society for Psychical Research on the phenomena shown by the medium, Mrs. Piper, especially in discussing the claim that a dead friend was trying to communicate, he reviews the entire evidence with the statement of a "felt conviction that somehow or somewhere there is a survival of individuality with the power to communicate with the living." It shows James as at once a rigidly empirical scientist and a mystic.

In the chapter on the will, he shows very much the same type of alternation with reference to the question whether effort is a mere muscular contraction or the immediate awareness of a deeper force. He gives a careful analysis of action as ideo-motor action and of control as consisting only in selecting the more pleasant end and attending to the idea that corresponds to it. Effort he shows to consist in nothing more than the sensations that arise from contracting muscles, some directly involved in the act and some contracting through chance spread of impulses. He was vigorous in rejecting Wundt's notion, held in his early period and later abandoned, that we are directly aware of motor nervous energy that is discharged to the muscles. It was Münsterberg's controversy with Wundt on this point that led James to secure the former's appointment at Harvard, as we shall see. Still James was so entirely averse to regarding mind as without efficacy in action, that he was ready to use the feeling that after all we do make real choices as justification for a reservation in his final conclusion that we need consider only the mental content. The apparent contradiction is no more than the recognition that one may and probably must assume two points of view. He takes one at one time and another at another. When he feels the need of justification, he ascribes one to science, the other to metaphysics. This would probably not justify the adoption of the two positions to a man who was looking for final truth, but does save James from any possible charge of being innocent of knowledge of the inconsistency.

James's attitude towards experimentation was an interesting illustration of a struggle between the new and the old. As a physiologist he did experiments on what would now be called psychological problems even before Wundt began his laboratory. On the whole he was impatient with much experimental work, and after he had established himself in psychology, always complained of being bored by directing students' work. After a long survey of Fechner's work on psychophysics, he concludes that the final outcome of the work is "just nothing." On the other hand, he makes much of the early memory work of Ebbinghaus and of the reaction-time work of the Wundt laboratory. He carried out a long experimental investigation of the results of memory-training with a negative outcome. This was the first actual experiment on the problem and started a long series with much controversy. In the *Talks to Teachers* he refers somewhat contemptuously to the "brass instrument psychology." It is again a question which of his moods we are to take seriously. On the whole it must be said that in his serious moods he uses and approves the experimental method, but would at times prefer to trust insight rather than go to the expense of time demanded for experimental verification.

James did much to make psychology popular in America. His clarity of style and his vivid figures always won attention and carried conviction to his readers. James was also immediately recognized abroad, especially by the English, French and Italians, a fact which called attention to the other American workers who came after him. The Gifford Lectures, later published as the *Varieties of Religious Experience,* had an even wider popular appeal than his more strictly psychological writings. His style was in marked contrast to that of his brother Henry, the novelist. Librarians were said to ask a reader who called for a book by James, whether he meant "the novelist who wrote psychology, or the psychologist who wrote novels." Taken all in all, James stands as the most vital of the American psychologists, and directly and indirectly had a profound influence upon the whole development of the science.

LADD

Of a different character was the contribution of George Trumbull Ladd (1842–1921) who began as a clergyman, came into psychology by way of theology and philosophy, and was Professor of Psychology at Yale from 1881 to 1905, when he retired. Ladd became acquainted with the work of the Germans relatively early through the writings of Wundt, and embodied them with his own conclusions in text-books. He gave a clear and systematic presentation that was very useful to the student. He also deserves credit for the establishment at Yale of one of the early psychological laboratories, under Scripture in 1892.

HALL

The great rise of interest in psychology in America came with the establishment of laboratories under the stimulus of the Wundtian School. The first was founded by Stanley Hall at Johns Hopkins University in 1881, when that University was established as a model of advanced instruction on the German plan for America. G. Stanley Hall was born in 1846 at Ashfield, Massachusetts, received the A.B. degree from Williams in 1867, and then was successively a tutor in a private family, a student at Union Theological Seminary in New York, and professor at Antioch College, 1871 to 1876. He then went abroad and studied for three years at Leipzig, Berlin and London. At Leipzig he came under the influence of Wundt, although he did most of his actual laboratory work with Ludwig in physiology. On his return to America, he was for a time Lecturer on Education at Harvard, and then was asked to become professor of philosophy at Johns Hopkins. While there he founded the *American Journal of Psychology*, the first journal in English devoted to psychology alone. In 1889 he was asked to become President of Clark University. Here he founded a second laboratory under the direction of E. C. Sanford, which was one of the most fertile in work in the early years of the science in America. Hall's interest turned to education soon after he went to Clark, and his publications were mostly in that field. He developed the method of the questionnaire, a service of doubtful value, even if he did make as much of it as it was possible to make. The founding of the first psychological laboratory and the first psychological journal in America are his most important achievements.

CATTELL

Another pioneer in American psychology is James McKeen Cattell. Born in 1860 at Easton, Pennsylvania, he studied at Lafayette College of which his father was president, and then in numerous European universities. From 1883 to 1886 he was a student at Leipzig and was Wundt's first assistant. After receiving his degree from Leipzig he worked with Galton at Cambridge, and for a year lectured there. He came to the University of Pennsylvania in 1889, where he started a laboratory, being the first man in America to hold a professorship specifically in psychology. He was called to Columbia in 1891 and founded the laboratory there, which has been one of the most fruitful in experimental work. Cattell's work with Wundt was in reaction-time and on the range of perception. Always inclined to the objective method, he when with Galton turned to a statistical interpretation of his results, and was one of the first to be interested in individual differences. He retired in 1917 to the management of his several periodicals in science and education.

OTHER PSYCHOLOGISTS

When the foundation of laboratories had once begun, it went on very quickly. Among the early students at Johns Hopkins, Bryan and Jastrow started laboratories in 1888, the one at Indiana, and the other at Wisconsin. Wolf, who had received his degree under Wundt, founded one in Nebraska in 1890. Frank Angell, also a student at Leipzig, began the laboratory at Cornell in 1891, and when he was called to Leland Stanford the next year, was succeeded by Titchener. In 1894 there were laboratories in twenty-seven universities and now no university or college of standing is without one. Many normal schools and other institutions for teachers have also introduced them. From that time on, the story becomes one of the development of methods, the accumulation of data, and the growth of schools of thought on fundamental topics, rather than one of the work of separate men.

We may make an exception in the case of Münsterberg, a picturesque character whose story is divided between two countries, Germany and America. Hugo

Münsterberg was born at Danzig in 1863. He studied with Wundt at Leipzig and received his degree of Ph.D., then studied medicine and was given the M. D. degree at Heidelberg. He went to Freiburg as *docent* and was made assistant professor. In 1892 he was invited at James's suggestion to be Professor of Experimental Psychology at Harvard for three years. At the end of the period he returned to Freiburg for two years and then came back to Harvard on a permanent appointment in 1897, remaining until his death in 1915.

One phase of his career throws an interesting light on the inconsistency of human nature—at least of Wundt's nature and his own—and brings out an important psychological attitude. In those early years Wundt believed that man was directly conscious of the discharge of motor energy to a muscle, that when a man moved a muscle he was aware of the motor nerve-current before it left the cortex, and that this constituted the consciousness of will. Wundt called this the "innervation sense." Münsterberg as a result of experiment and observation decided that everything favored the view that all appreciation of movement arose from the stimulation of the sensory nerves in the muscles while the movement was being executed. He presented his results as a dissertation for his degree and Wundt refused to accept it. He substituted for it one entitled "The Doctrine of Natural Adaptation" which was sufficiently colorless to arouse no opposition. After he had become established at Freiburg, he published an expanded form of his original dissertation as *Die Willenshandlung* (Voluntary Action) and contested the reality of will as well as direct awareness of its action. It is somewhat interesting as an indication of the vanity of controversy, that Wundt in a later edition of his work shifted to what was practically Münsterberg's position, and that Münsterberg himself made much in his last writings of the direct awareness of the motor discharge. The two who had fought each other so bitterly on the point both reversed themselves and finally fought from opposite sides of the same question.

Münsterberg came to his second position indirectly as an extension of the Jamesian back-stroke theory of emotions. He found that much of the consciousness that attaches to many mental processes or general reactions comes from the muscles that are active during these processes. Thence he made the next step, that this consciousness arises from the excitation of the motor neurones which initiate the contraction. This he called the action theory. As applied, it would mean that when one sees an object the perception depends not primarily upon the arousal of sensory nerve elements, but upon the motor elements which are aroused reflexly and which will in time produce the movements appropriate to the situation. This is little more than the extension of the "innervation sense."

Münsterberg's last position is an anticipation of one

of the last German movements, in so far as it opposes to the ordinary analytic and dynamic explanation in psychology a second which undertakes merely to appreciate mental processes. He would divide psychology into two parts, a causal psychology which seeks to refer each mental event to other mental and physical events, and an evaluating psychology which regards mental events as the expression of a pure soul and attempts only to appreciate them with reference to definite moral and aesthetic ends. The two sciences must run parallel to each other, but one cannot mix them nor pass from one to the other. The division seems to be a result of the desire to take two opposing attitudes towards mental phenomena. It makes explicit the inconsistencies implicit in James's treatment, in so far as he gave a completely scientific explanation of self and the voluntary processes, but at the end never seemed quite satisfied to stop his treatment there.

J. Mark Baldwin should be mentioned among the men who aided in developing an interest in psychology in America. Born in 1861 at Columbia, South Carolina, he graduated from Princeton and studied in Germany. He was professor successively at Lake Forest, Toronto, Princeton, and Johns Hopkins, until he retired to live in Paris in 1909. He started the *Psychological Review* with Cattell, in 1894, which has been the parent of a whole group of more specialized publications in psychology. He wrote a number of text-books in the early days. More original was his *Mental Development* which applied Tarde's theory of imitation to explain the results obtained from studying his young daughter. *Thought and Things* should also be mentioned as a contribution to the psychology of reasoning. He did much as an organizer, and also furthered the functional and evolutionary attitude towards psychology.

Recent American psychology has been marked by greater extension of experimental work upon the older problems. Most characteristic was the development of animal psychology and of practical psychology. The work with tests began soon after Binet formulated his methods and was applied to all sorts of capacities and accomplishments. The most striking single development was the application of group tests of intelligence to men drafted for the European war in 1917–18. Then there has been a considerable development in the application of psychological principles to industry. These we need no more than mention, but a statement of American contributions to psychology would not be complete without them.

JOHN B. WATSON   SIGMUND FREUD
Courtesy Horace Liveright, Inc.

ALFRED ADLER   WOLFGANG KÖHLER
Courtesy Greenberg, Inc.

FOUR MODERN PSYCHOLOGISTS

CHAPTER XV

THE DEVELOPMENT OF ABNORMAL PSYCHOLOGY

A N interesting and in many ways a very curious chapter of modern psychology is that which has grown out of the study of mental abnormalities. It is not only important for itself but has had a very marked influence upon the development of certain ideas concerning normal processes. Its theories have been taken up by the layman and applied in sociology, and in education, and in the interpretation of biographies. The beginnings of this modern theory can be seen in Mesmer, a Viennese physician of the latter half of the eighteenth century, who became the talk of the hour in Paris just before the French Revolution. He applied the notion of Paracelsus that man is influenced by the heavenly bodies and by magnets, and combined it with certain practical methods of casting out devils hit upon by Gassner, a Swabian priest, to produce trances in his patients. In practice Mesmer would make passes over the body of a client, and when the patient went into a trance would give him suggestions for the cure of his ailment. Mesmer was investigated by a committee of the French Academy, including Franklin, then the American Ambassador in Paris. They reported that the trance was all imagination, since they showed conclusively that magnetism had nothing to do with it. They did not ask how imagination could produce a trance. With the outbreak of the French Revolution interest in the phenomenon ceased, and Mesmerism or animal magnetism was used only by charlatans for half a century.

Scientific investigation of the trance began in 1843, with Braid, an English surgeon, who became convinced that it was a real physiological condition resulting from fatigue of the frontal lobes of the brain. To Braid we owe the name hypnotism which replaced that of animal magnetism. Braid's work became known in France through Dr. Azam of Bordeaux, who reported one of the first cases of alternating personality. Dr. Azam appreciated the similarity between hypnotism, hysteria, and his case of alternating personality. Thus several further developments took place; for Broca, the discoverer of aphasia, became acquainted with Azam's work, and called it to the notice of Charcot, the head of the Salpétrière in Paris and the recognized authority in nervous diseases. Charcot had been devoting himself to the study of hysteria and took up the investigation of hypnotism with great energy. He believed that the two conditions had much in common, that only hysterical cases could be hypnotized, and that their symptoms could be modified by hypnotism. While his work with hypnotism started a controversy with a school of men at Nancy who had been carrying on investigations based on another theory, and who were probably more nearly correct in their conclusions, the weight of his name gave hypnotism scientific recognition. This acceptance was sealed when he was permitted to read a paper on the subject before the French Academy.

More important than his indorsement of hypnotism was the trend that Charcot gave to the study and treatment of hysteria, for from it have grown practically all of the theories of abnormal psychology which we have today. Charcot recognized hysteria as a functional disease of the nervous system, that is, a disease due to improper action of an organ that was normal in structure. He opposed functional diseases to the organic nervous diseases in which destruction or alteration of the tissues could be shown. From Charcot at least two important types of theory developed.

JANET

The direct line of descent is to be traced mainly through Pierre Janet. Janet was born in Paris in 1859, a nephew of Paul Janet, the philosopher. He studied at the *École Normale* and received his *agrégé*, which entitled him to teach, in 1881. He taught philosophy for a time and was given his *docteur ès lettres* in 1889. He then became interested in medicine, studied in the medi-

cal school and was given the M.D. in 1894. He lectured
at the Sorbonne and at the Salpétrière where he had a
clinic until 1902, when he was made professor at the
Collège de France. Meantime he carried on an extensive
private practice in nervous diseases.

Janet regards all of the psycho-neuroses as due to a
weakening of nervous activity, a reduction in the
amount of nervous energy at the command of the
patient. This is the predisposing cause. In an individual
of this type one of two diseases may make its appearance. In the first, hysteria, there occurs a dissociation,
an actual splitting of the normal bonds of consciousness. The split comes as the result of an emotional
or physical shock, usually prepared for by some long
struggle or series of conflicts. Janet cites a typical case
in which a patient after the death of his wife has a
bitter quarrel with his mother-in-law over the possession of his child. As a consequence, he loses in his ordinary state all memory of the quarrel and of his child.
In addition he suffers from a complete paralysis and
must lie in bed. "In the middle of the night he rises
slowly, jumps lightly out of bed—for the paralysis we
have spoken of has quite vanished—takes his pillow
and hugs it. We know by his countenance and his words
that he mistakes this pillow for his child, and that he
believes he is saving his child from his mother-in-law.
Then, bearing that weight, he opens the door and runs
through the courtyard; climbing to the housetop he runs

all about the buildings of the hospital with marvellous agility. One must take great care to get him down, for he wakes with a stupefied air, and as soon as he is awake, both his legs are paralyzed again, and he must be carried to his bed. He does not remember his escape and wonders how it happens that people were obliged to go to the top of the house for a poor man who has been paralyzed in his bed for a month." [1] Thus there is complete dissociation between the event that causes the hysteria and the daily life of the patient. When later he recalls the occasion of the disease, he forgets his daily life of the present. The paralysis in this case and many sensory disturbances seem to be due, according to Janet, to the fact that control of the member remains with the ideas that have been forgotten. It is as if the patient had forgotten his leg. Similarly, a person may be totally blind although the visual reflexes are retained, or anaesthetic on a large part of the skin although there is no sign of degeneration of the nerves that supply the parts. The sensations penetrate only to the split-off portion of consciousness and so have no effect upon the part of the cortex that is dominant at the time. Hysteria is a phenomenon of dissociation of consciousness, with the control of the individual alternating between the two portions. The disturbances of the so-called resting stage are due to the fact that control of the paralyzed member or of the anaesthetic skin is exercised

[1] Major Symptoms of Hysteria, p. 29.

by a group of ideas not dominant at the moment.

The other form of psycho-neurosis, which Janet calls psychasthenia, is characterized by a lowering of the mental energy without dissociation. The patient misinterprets the situation or cannot control his ideas sufficiently. This disease is marked by failure to recognize situations. Either all objects, new as well as old, seem familiar, or nothing is recognized, all is strange. The patient cannot bring himself to perform the simplest act. He will stand half an hour before a door and be unable to open it. Or he is obsessed by the idea that something will happen to him. He fears that he may contract some disease if he comes into the slightest contact with other persons, or he fears that his hands are dirty, no matter how recently he has washed, and must perform the act again. Or he is afraid of open places (agoraphobia), or of closed places (claustrophobia). Again these patients suffer from impulsions, they fear that they must perform some act that is repulsive to them. A barber develops the fear that he will cut the throat of his client, although he dreads nothing so much, and the impulsion forces him to abandon his trade. Janet would explain all these symptoms on the assumption that control of acts or of ideas demands a certain minimum of mental energy which these patients do not possess. Consciousness is spread too thin in these cases, as in hysteria it is too restricted in area, so that parts of the nervous system are there compelled to go unnoticed. As evidence of the narrowing of consciousness in hysteria, Janet cites cases in which cure of paralysis of one leg will at once bring on paralysis of the other. He asserts that it is like sleeping under a blanket that is too short, which, if one pulls it up to cover the neck, leaves the feet uncovered: if the physician cures paralysis of one arm it appears in the other, if he cures blindness in one eye, the other becomes blind.

Janet's theory gives a good description of the fact, but it is lacking in an adequate dynamic explanation. Even granting that consciousness is an entity the amount of which can be reduced, why and how it should be dissociated, and why thinning it should produce an obsession, is not quite clear. Later theories have sought a more specifically causal explanation.

FREUD

The great rival to Janet's explanation was suggested by Sigmund Freud, a physician in Vienna. Freud was born at Freiberg in Moravia in 1856. He was the son of an old man by a young second wife, and his early life seems to have been full of the jealousies that he makes so much of in his explanations of disease. He moved to Vienna when a boy of four, and was educated in a *Gymnasium* and the University of that city. After receiving his M.D. he worked in psychiatry and nervous anatomy in the clinic of the university. He was one of the first to make experiments on the properties of cocaine, and after discovering its nature he had the idea of suggesting its availability as an anaesthetic in operations on the eyes. He neglected to publish or test the idea, however, and Koller, a young colleague, on reading Freud's report at once made the practical application and became the pioneer in the field. This seems to have caused Freud lasting regret.

Freud received the great impetus to his work in neurology from a winter spent with Charcot in Paris in 1885–86. He there absorbed the notion that hysteria was of mental origin. On his return he translated Charcot's works into German and associated himself with an older physician, Breuer, in the study and treatment of the neuroses. At first they used hypnotism, but later developed the method of psycho-analysis, a method of continued questioning. At this point in his career he split off from Charcot and Janet and developed his own school. He was not for long associated with the university but gathered his disciples in a room in his own house where cases were discussed and his theories developed.

We can perhaps make clearer Freud's theory by describing his first famous case, which he treated with Breuer. Single cases play a great rôle in the development of a theory of the neuroses. If an early case is striking in its character and is successfully treated, it tends to mould the attitude towards the disease as a whole. It becomes the type and an attempt is made to fit all others into its pattern. The patient in this case was a young girl who developed an inability to drink, and also to speak German, as well as a paralysis of the extremities and anaesthesias of the skin. When questioned in hypnosis she told of her English governess whom she disliked and of an occasion when she saw the governess's dog drinking out of a glass. "After she has given energetic expression to her restrained anger, she asked for a drink, drank a large quantity of water without difficulty, and woke from hypnosis with the glass at her lips. The symptoms thereupon vanished immediately"; also her knowledge of German came back. The incapacity to speak anything but English had been due to fixation on the governess. On the basis of this cure by recall of the disagreeable experience which had been the cause of the symptom, Freud substituted his psycho-analytical method generally for hypnosis and the older methods. As he said at the time, patients of this type suffered from pathogenic memories, which trouble the sick because they are unwilling to face them. Could the painful memories only be brought to full consciousness, the disease symptoms would disappear.

As time went on, Freud made the type of memory that was capable of producing a disease more and more special, and also developed an original theory of mind which explained the effect ascribed to the memories. One phase of Freud's system may be said to have been derived from Schopenhauer, as his notion of disease came from Charcot. Schopenhauer asserted that the determining force in man, as in the universe, is a Will which pervades every man as it does the world as a whole. It is not known to the individual but lies deep in the unconscious and its effects are assumed to be the result of the desires of the individual himself. Man knows what he is doing but not why. Schopenhauer was a pessimist and believed that the unconscious Will delighted in seeing man suffer and so drove him to all the acts that would cause him pain. Freud took over the notion of the unconscious, without making it specifically will. He asserts that man's mental life is divided into two parts, the conscious life that we know and an unconsciousness that we do not know, but which is pictured as just as much an individual as the normal self, with desires and memories of its own.

Freud did not give his unconscious the blind malevolence of Schopenhauer's. Instead, he thought of it as the embodiment of the fundamental instincts of the race, especially of the sex instincts, and perennially bent on keeping sex ideas and impulses before the consciousness. He called the sex impulse libido, and made it the one important drive in life. He thinks of the consciousness as having a censor that has been developed through living in a conventional and somewhat puritanical society, and that the main object of the unconscious is to outwit this censor. The unconscious may take advantage of moments when consciousness is weak, as during sleep, to force its libidinous thoughts upon the upper self. Even then, however, it finds it necessary to veil them in symbols if it is to get them past the gate. One might question on *a priori* grounds why the unconscious should not prefer to enjoy these thoughts by itself and not endeavor to force them upon an unwilling upper self. Apparently, however, the unconscious is a social being and must share its delights.

The neuroses, according to Freud, arise because of the struggle between the unconscious and the conscious. The constant thwarting of the desires of the unconscious leads to their being satisfied through disease. Freud does not classify the neuroses as so distinctly separate in character and causation as Janet does. Janet's hysteria he calls a conversion neurosis, for in it the unconscious attains its end by transforming its wishes into physical ailments. When unpleasant sights are thrust continually upon the patient, he unconsciously escapes them by becoming blind. When walking would lead to disagreeable consequences, he unconsciously escapes from them by becoming paralyzed. In a second form, the compulsion neurosis, the unconscious keeps its wish before the conscious by forcing it to think of doing something which is symbolic of its desires, even if it alone knows what the symbol signifies. Or the individual suffers from an idea that he cannot be rid of, and which always gives pain, although its connection with the real thought of the unconscious is but slight. Again, in the anxiety neurosis, the third type, the patient always worries over something although the object of the dread is not the thing that is represented. All three forms of neurosis have the same general cause. The expression alone is different.

Freud fairly early came to the notion that the repressed idea or event was always sexual in origin. When it appeared that many of the instances seemed to come from very early childhood, before the sex impulses were supposed to have developed, Freud found preliminaries of sex activities in thumb-sucking and similar apparent enjoyment of parts of the body. As time went on he made more of these early incidents and finally developed a full history, or perhaps better a mythology, of sex. The child is at first in love only with his own body: narcissism. This may be transferred to the body of another of the same sex: homosexuality. Also every child is from birth always sexually in love with the parent of the opposite sex and hates the parent of the same sex: the Œdipus complex, named from the old Greek myth. If the individual is to be happily married, he must if a boy, find a mate who resembles his mother; if a girl, one who resembles her father. All these statements are based upon the interpretations of the histories or the explanations of the dreams of patients. In his findings Freud had to trust to a patient's memory regarding what happened before he was a year old, in many cases much before. It must be said that to an outsider many of Freud's conclusions seem to be based on the assumption that if you can't prove that they are false, they must be true.

The method Freud used when he gave up hypnosis was merely to ask the patient to relax as much as possible and then say anything that came into his mind. When in his confession the patient hit upon an idea that was pathogenic, the emotional cause of the disease, he would have a crisis of emotion with the passing of which he would be relieved. The ordinary course was for the emotion attached to the original event to be transferred to the physician—the patient would, for example, if his trouble had been caused by a love-affair, fall in love with him, and then the cure could not be completed until the emotion was sublimated—in such a case, that is, until love of the physician was replaced by some high ideal of an impersonal character which might absorb the personal emotion. This method Freud called psycho-analysis.

Freud's theory of dreams must also be taken into account in explaining and understanding the practice of psycho-analysis. A dream is always the expression of a suppressed wish, and the wish must always be sexual in character. Since the real content of the dream would be offensive to the censor, it can be expressed only in symbolic form, and to understand the real wish, one must translate these symbols into the underlying desire. When a woman dreamed that she had wrung the neck of a white dog, it was found that she had quarrelled with her sister-in-law and ended by saying "Get out, I cannot bear the sight of a barking dog in my house." In her dream she confused the enemy with the dog, and permitted herself to dream of wringing its neck, symbolizing the desire to be rid of her enemy. In the treatment, the patient is encouraged to remember carefully all dreams and write them down on waking. Then they serve as introduction to the questioning in psycho-analysis that is to produce the cure. On the theory, it is really not difficult to discover what the symbols signify, since in normal individuals they always have reference to the opposite sex. A dictionary of these symbols has been prepared, but it is not necessary provided the analyst knows the sex of the dreamer.

Freud is not content with explaining dreams alone, but every chance remark of the individual, every accident, even every bit of wit he sees as the expression of the deliberate will of the unconscious. In his *Psychopathology of Every Day Life* he points out that when a person drops a dish and breaks it, if he will search his memory long enough, he will find that the dish had been given him by an enemy or was associated with some unpleasant event which caused the unconscious desire to remove it from sight. Freud asserts that no act of man occurs without deliberate intention and, when no intent is known in the conscious, the unconscious must be acting and concealing the motive. Thus Freud's theory is not merely an explanation of disease, but is a complete psychology and a somewhat pessimistic philosophy of life.

Freud's doctrine was variously received in various circles, and has been for two or three decades the center of a controversy between devout apostles and scoffing opponents. He had a small following at home, but not in academic circles. In England and America, especially in America, the clinicians tended to accept him, if with modifications, while the psychologists were mostly incredulous. In France, the older Charcot school and Janet held the field, so that Freud's doctrine made little headway, and in Germany there were far more scoffers than followers. Gradually its admitted practitioners are becoming fewer and fewer, and the ardor of those who were disciples is cooling. The numerous cases of war shock, that were fundamentally hysterical or neurotic in character, tended to reduce the importance of the sex element in Freud's argument. At first Freud attempted to assert that the accidents of war had their effect only because they were sex symbols or revived old sex conflicts, but this was a little too absurd. Nevertheless psychoanalysis has had the effect of giving a more important place to the psychological attitude towards nervous diseases, and of emphasizing the fact that a patient's old conflicts and present emotional shocks are important factors in the development of neuroses. It stands as a strange episode in the history of psychology but one that has not been without many beneficial by-products.

JUNG AND ADLER

Freud had many followers who developed modifications of their own. One of the better known and less extravagant is Jung, a physician of Zurich. Jung kept Freud's term libido as a designation of sexual desire, but weakened the sexual reference, making it mean any strong instinctive impulse, although he regarded sex as one of the strongest. He also believed that the unconscious in any one individual was identical with the unconscious of all other men. In this he was more like Schopenhauer, so far as he assumes a race unconscious that finds expression in each individual. The common knowledge of the race may also be detected in the psycho-analysis of a patient. He argues from this that myths are but symbols of the overweening desires of the race, and they attract the masses because the unconscious of each man appreciates the symbolic meaning of the tale, although the upper consciousness is unaware of it.

Jung also deserves mention for suggesting the division of all individuals into two great classes according as they are mainly concerned with themselves or with the world about them. The former belong in the class of introverts and are always self-centred, more interested in their own emotions and in the interpretation they put upon events than they are in the events themselves. The others constitute the extraverts, who are objective in their attitudes, interpreting men and things for themselves rather than for the emotions they arouse. The distinction is useful so far, but Jung complicates it by having the unconscious take the attitude that the conscious rejects. Thus the conscious extravert is an unconscious introvert, for his unconscious stores up all the subjective reactions that his conscious denies him. This revelling in the subjective on the part of the unconscious tends to produce hysteria, which according to Jung is always a disease of the extravert. The introvert is subject to other types of neuroses, for he is willing to admit that he is interested in himself and does not so completely suppress his complexes.

Another important follower of Freud who modified his theory noticeably is Alfred Adler. Also a physician in Vienna, Adler at first accepted Freud's notions completely, then gradually modified them in his own way. Adler would replace the sex factor, according to Freud always dominant in the disturbing complex, by the complex of inferiority. He believes that every neurosis has its origin in a feeling of inferiority on the part of the patient. The fundamental cause of the feeling is that the patient sets an ideal for himself that is higher than he can attain and struggles vainly to reach it. Sometimes the feeling is due to a loss or failure in some organ, sometimes it is purely a matter of disproportion between goal and achievement because the goal is set too high. Adler brings in the sex element as subordinate. He believes that every woman has an inferiority complex because she is not a man, and that many men have one because they do not sufficiently dominate some woman. The results are frequently manifest in a too great self-assertion in the endeavor to make up for the felt insufficiency. The relations of conscious and unconscious, the efficiency of symbols and the interpretations of dreams are retained from Freud. The feeling of inferiority is merely added to the other Freudian explanations.

CHAPTER XVI

MODERN SCHOOLS OF PSYCHOLOGY: STRUC-
TURALISM AND FUNCTIONALISM

THE present probably exhibits a wider range of diversity in the theories of what mental processes are, whether they exist and, if they do not exist, what psychology really should discuss, than any preceding age. These theories range from making mental states alone the object of investigation, to denying the existence of mental states altogether. Some, as we have just seen, would find the essentials of mind in the unconscious, others would find them in the physical organism, and others would contend that we should not bother with the essentials at all but should restrict ourselves to a study of the surface phenomena alone. We can best present these various theories of psychology by grouping their representatives into fairly well recognized schools and mentioning only the most striking figures in each.

We may content ourselves with a statement of the more important tenets of the six following schools:

1) The structuralist school, which holds that consciousness is directly observable and is composed of

simple, definitely describable elements. For this school the task of psychology is to discover and describe each of these elements, and to determine how they combine to produce the more complicated structures.

2) The functionalist school, which would study not the contents but the capacities of mind, not what it is, but what it does. In its usual form this school is interested not in the functions of mind alone, but in the mental functions of the organism as a whole.

3) The behavioristic school, which contends that consciousness has no existence, and that psychology should study only the actions of an organism, and that only from the outside, in another individual.

4) The hormic school, which holds that all is conation or will, that man's consciousness is dominated by ends and these ends control consciousness even before we are aware of them.

5) The *Gestalt* school, which accepts consciousness as the material for study, but insists that we know only forms or wholes in consciousness, that its elements do not exist, or exist only in relation to the larger wholes that dominate them.

6) The understanding psychology, which would give over all attempt to analyze consciousness or explain it causally, and be content to appreciate it and its ends.

These are but samples of what seem to be the more important schools of the present. One could add nearly as many more if one would recognize certain groups of

men who limit their explanations to a few special points, or who present minor modifications of certain of the main tendencies.

The structuralist psychology is the simplest of any of these and is most closely related to the older doctrine. It is not very different from the position held by Wundt on the one side, and by the Mills on the other. Its most prominent recent representative, Edward Bradford Titchener, was born at Chichester, England, in 1867, and educated at Malvern College and Oxford University, from which he received the A.B. in 1890. He studied under Wundt in Leipzig and received his Ph.D. in 1892. He came immediately to Cornell University, became active in building up the laboratory and continued there until his death in 1927. Titchener's most characteristic belief was a faith that mental processes are real and more or less persistent entities, with fixed qualities and other attributes, and that they may be studied and catalogued as the systematic botanist describes and classifies his plants, or the chemist analyzes his substances into a limited number of known elements that always combine in the same ways to give specific substances. At first Titchener followed Mill in accepting definitely the chemical analogy. Especially he believed that mental combinations were like chemical compounds in that a compound did not by mere inspection reveal its components, for the qualities of the elements were lost in those of the compound. In 1909, however, he abandoned the analogy, but not the fundamental attitude upon which it was based.

Titchener relied wholly upon introspection to determine his elements and their qualities. He experimented only to give the subject, whom he always called the observer, an opportunity to watch the mental states and processes under controlled conditions. In the experiment one should note and describe all sensations received and all memory processes added, refer them to the sense organ, note the succession of mental states, and give any incidental phenomena that seemed relevant. The object was to determine how many kinds of sensations there are and how many attributes can be ascribed to them. Titchener was interested in determining how memory images differ from sensations, how ideas follow each other, how concepts differ in their imagery from sensations or memories and what makes them concepts. With his students, especially Geissler, he conducted a long experiment to determine how many different levels of clearness may be present in consciousness at one time, and how they change. This investigation arose from Wundt's assumption that one has a point of clearest vision in the center of consciousness, and a field of vaguer consciousness round about. It ended with the conclusion that different individuals have different numbers of steps of clearness.

Titchener was not willing to discuss the nervous system, on the assumption that it was properly the topic of the physiologist. While he was convinced that brain and mind were closely connected and was willing to make hypotheses as to nervous correlates of mental states, he always kept his treatment very vague. This included an unwillingness to coördinate the discussion of the mental antecedents of movement with the neurological processes that immediately evoked the muscular contraction. He gave a complete description of the ideas that preceded, followed and accompanied the act, but gave little attention to the physiological phase of the process.

He was little interested in the function of the images in the knowing process. His percept was complete when he had described the sensations and the images that they evoked. More especially in his discussion of meaning in the thinking process, he stopped with the description of the images which were in consciousness when an object was represented or meant. The meaning of the idea was just another image, and he did not seem to think that the meaning might be anything different from the image. He even specifically denied that one had a right to consider in psychology the relation between the object that was represented and the mental process which represented it. The relation was to be considered only to make sure that the psychologist did not confuse the object represented or intended with the mere mental content. To mix the thing meant with the image was to commit the "stimulus error" and this must be avoided at all hazard. This was a highly desirable caution, but in

Titchener's case care on that point seems to have prevented any examination of the problem of representation itself.

While structuralism narrowed the field of psychology considerably, the work done by this school was extremely important and must be taken into account by those who approach the subject from any point of view. The work which Titchener did or stimulated his students to do was always very thorough, and much of it would not have been undertaken on the presuppositions of any other school. The sharp criticism to which other schools were being subjected exerted a tonic influence on workers of all schools which held them to a high standard. The net result was a gain to the science.

THE FUNCTIONALIST SCHOOL

Probably the most conservative in the modern group is the functionalist school. It is more conservative than others in that it excludes from discussion fewer of the topics that naturally fall within psychology, and commits itself in advance less definitely to any particular interpretation. For this reason it has had a wide following. The functionalist school is a logical outcome of James's somewhat catholic position, and while he was not himself counted a functionalist, his theories influenced its development and its adherents found a warrant for certain of their beliefs in his works. They took comfort in his pragmatism as an underlying philosophy.

The accepted functionalism rests primarily upon biology. The function that interested its early adherents was the capacity of the animal to adapt itself in the environment, and mind was the sum total of the capacities that made such adaptation possible. One could perfectly well apply the term to mean a study of the functions of consciousness apart from the mental states that conceivably make these accomplishments possible. For after all we can be more certain, and usually are more certain, what a mental process means for us and what it makes possible in the way of knowledge, than we are of what it is in itself.

The first specific statement of the functionalist position was given by John Dewey in an article in the Psychological Review for 1896, entitled "The Reflex Arc Concept." In this he tried to link the simple physiological notion of the reflex with the wider environment of the movement on the one hand, and with the needs of the reacting individual on the other. Each reflex arc should not be considered for itself alone, but as growing out of preceding reactions and interpretations. It was ordinarily asserted that a stimulus or sensation causes a movement, and assumed that nothing else was needed for the explanation. Dewey insisted that all parts were closely linked together, that the sensation develops with reference to the movement as well as being the cause of the muscular contraction. Again, the kinaesthetic sensations which result from the moving muscle are also important in the total complex. They constitute an important element in appreciating the success of the movement, and tie it back to the purpose from which the chain of acts started. They also serve to start new movements when suitable stimuli appear.

Dewey urged that the psychologist should consider the entire process of coördinating the organism with the momentary situation in the environment, and that sensation and movement are important only as they contribute to that end. Each must be studied but it must be studied in its relations to the other. The unitary act completes a circle from a sensation as part of a situation, through movement, to a new sensation that arises out of the movement. The movement and the appreciation of the movement modify the environment, and the new situation which arises must again be appreciated and new movements initiated in the light of that new situation and the purpose to be attained, which is again constantly being modified by each movement. Dewey used the term function to indicate the end and its attainment, and this apparently gave the name to the school.

With this article as a text, James Angell and his students at Chicago extended the definition and explanation of psychology in terms of its functions. In a presidential address before the Psychological Association in 1907, Angell states that "functionalism is a study of the responses of the whole individual, rather than an investigation of the movements of any single part of an individual." The functionalist school is more biological in attitude than any of its predecessors, in so far as it deals with the organism as a unit, including both body and mind, and not with either body or mind alone. It suggests that it might study mind or mental process as an instrument by which the organism adapts itself to variations in the environment; or, if we omit the term mind, it is a study of the means by which an animal adapts itself. It is, to differentiate psychology from physiology, a study of those reactions of man or animal which cannot be interpreted in a strictly mechanical way. In so far as it deals with consciousness it is more interested in the uses and meanings of the states than in the states themselves. It concerns itself with the aims and ends that are accomplished, not with elements and attributes. Angell suggested that we could use the output of work or the ability to recall an event, without being in the least concerned with the nature of mental images.

However, the functionalists were not ready to give up introspection. They would make all possible use of that tool within its proper field. Mental imagery should be studied, for it may modify function and is always interesting in itself; in consequence there is every reason why psychology should take account of it. While mental states are not permanent but merely the transient accompaniments of neural changes, they nevertheless give an indication of the changing conditions of the organism that nothing can replace. If they had no value for themselves, they would deserve study for the light they throw on the activity of nerves. The fact that they tend to be reinstated also gives a record of the past of the organism that is of the highest value. Functions must be the main object of study for psychology, but functions depend on mental processes and these must be studied if we are to understand the functions.

In actual practice, the functionalist investigates very much the same sort of problem as the structuralist. He is not so limited in his interpretation of the problems, for on the one hand he is willing to go beyond the mental state to consider the brain processes that are related to it, and on the other he interests himself in the meanings and other functions of the mental states. He has always recognized the physiological aspects of mental problems, and been much more biologically minded than the structuralist. On the whole, however, he differs from him in greater open mindedness towards the aims of the science, rather than in the material studied or the method by which it should be investigated. This catholicity of treatment led Titchener, in one of his last articles, to reject structuralism as too colorless. But this very colorlessness means inclusiveness, which is possibly the most desirable characteristic of a psychological system at the present.

CHAPTER XVII

ANIMAL PSYCHOLOGY AND BEHAVIORISM

A PHASE of investigation in psychology which has had great influence upon the development of recent schools of psychology is the study of the behavior of animals. All through the development of general psychology and biology there has been much mention of the mental processes of animals and discussion of the similarities between animal capacities and man's. Aristotle arranged his souls in series: the plant soul, which controls nutritive functions alone, the animal soul with its added capacity for motion and sensitivity, and the human soul which possesses reason in addition to all the other functions. Descartes opposed animals to man as being purely mechanical in their functions while man has a soul. Whether animals can reason has been a subject of discussion by the sciences and by the popular mind through the ages. Usually, it must be said, the discussions have begun with no attempt to define what is meant by reason. It is frequently asserted that man has reason, while the animal has only instinct, again with no attempt to define what is meant by instinct. Lack of definition of the terms and refraining from experiment or even careful observation has made all this discussion particularly futile.

Observations on animals were reported in sufficient detail to form the basis of scientific conclusions by Bonnet in the eighteenth century, and by Huber, Fabre, Forel, and Father Wassmann in the early nineteenth. The careful work of these men was all on insects and mostly on ants. The conclusions reached were colored by the preconceptions of the workers, but the observations themselves were carefully made and furnished data for decisions on many of the problems raised later. The writers themselves were concerned mainly with the question of the relative importance of instinct and reason in the animals.

At the end of the nineteenth century such work took a more specific turn. In 1883, Romanes published *Mental Evolution in Animals*, which, while largely developed on the basis of anecdotes found in literature and supplied by friends, was very acute in interpretation and written from the standpoint of a well-trained biologist. He was seeking evidence for the doctrine of evolution, especially for proof that human intelligence was derived from animal intelligence. More completely experimental was the work of Jacques Loeb, and more definite the conclusions. He may be said to have begun in 1888 the modern movement that seeks to explain in chemical terms the activities of animals. Loeb began as a plant physiologist and as such was a student of tropisms, which he explained as due to the chemical and physical effects of the stimulus upon the protoplasm. Then he noted that lower animals made movements under the same stimuli in much the same way as plants and extended his explanation to them. He named the various responses tropisms also; heliotropism for the effect of light, stereotropism for turning towards a solid body, etc. Verworn later studied the same processes and came to much the same conclusion, although, since he began with freely moving animals, he called the responses taxes, since they had a tendency to arrange themselves with reference to certain stimuli. Both Loeb and Verworn would explain all the responses by mechanical forces alone with no reference to mental characteristics.

Before this extreme chemical theory became widely known, experimental work had been begun by the psychologists. The earliest to make actual experiments, even if on a small scale, was Lloyd Morgan. In his *Animal Life and Intelligence,* published in 1896, he reports numerous experiments on young fowl and various animals. He is interested in tracing the development of behavior from the simplest response to stimulation, through instinct to the highest or rational forms of behavior. He is deserving of credit for urging what he calls the law of parsimony in the interpretation of all mental phenomena in animals, meaning that one should ascribe to an animal no higher mental processes than the minimum required to explain what is observed.

On this basis he granted to the higher animals intelligence defined as the ability to profit by chance responses made without rational foresight. From his animal work he developed later the philosophical doctrine of emergent evolution, which has attracted wide attention.

Possibly the turning point in the development of animal psychology came with the publication of Thorndike's *Animal Intelligence*, in 1898. Its conclusions and methods are not so different from Lloyd Morgan's as to be revolutionary, but the interpretations given and their wide acceptance marked the beginning of a new attitude and a new type of theory. Thorndike's work also spurred many to repeat and enlarge upon it, so that it initiated a new branch of work. He conducted experiments on cats and dogs by putting them in boxes with special devices closing the doors and studied the methods they used to escape. He found that they would learn to open a simple catch only after numerous trials and failures, and when they succeeded by chance, they could not at once repeat the successful movement. Thorndike's conclusion was that the animal made his movements as the results of some chance stimulus which happened to be present and that the success was entirely accidental. Then, when the desirable end had been attained, the animal recognized it and made attempts to repeat the correct movement. Plotting the curve of the time required for successful solving of the problem showed that progress was very slow, but that the learning would gradually be completed was shown by the fact that the movement would be made at once when the situation was presented. While Bain had indicated that learning in the child and in the animal took place by this process of trial and error, he had not drawn the general conclusions from it that Thorndike did, nor did he gain the same degree of acceptance for the theory.

The great value of the theory lay in the fact that it provided an explanation of animal activities that did not assign any special efficacy to consciousness in advance of the movement, and required only that a pleasant result should lead to repetition, after the movement had been executed by chance. It provided for the attainment of ends without the special intervention of an intention of attaining that end, and without making consciousness more than minimally important in the total process. The notion proved very fruitful in animal work and has been extended in several ways into human psychology. It makes it possible to derive complicated learning from spontaneous movements and thus to avoid ascribing to the animal any high mental capacity. Thorndike would deny the existence in animals of intentional imitation and all abstract thought. His theory thus greatly simplifies the schema for animal life and makes possible a similar reduction in the apparent complexity of human action.

This work started a flood of investigations in animal behavior, which, in America at least, in volume rivalled those on man. A little later investigations of intelligence became much in vogue, so that a foreign psychologist remarked on his return after a sojourn in America that the symbols for American psychology should be the white rat and the I. Q. (Intelligence Quotient). All the experimenters reached approximately the same conclusion—that all initial successes came through chance and were stamped in through the satisfaction derived from the reward that followed and the repetitions of the movement which that satisfaction induced. Only recently has it been objected that the assumption of a preliminary disposition prevents the explanation from being sufficiently mechanical. This objection seems to rest only upon the assumption that the word trial implies that the animal has an end in view, which was probably not in the least intended by Thorndike and does not seem to follow from the word itself. One other principle which was laid down by these early workers also proved important in later work in other fields, namely, that the psychologist should not speculate as to what the nature of its mental states may be when the animal performs any movement. These cannot by any chance be determined, and it is of no use to raise questions which cannot be answered. On the contrary, one may hope some day to determine what the nervous processes involved are and should be permitted to make hypotheses concerning them, even if the hypotheses cannot be immediately confirmed or rejected.

Jennings extended these methods of investigation to the simplest unicellular organisms. The results are published in his famous book, *The Behavior of the Lowest Organisms*. He showed that these lowest organisms follow in a considerable degree the same laws of action as the cat or the dog. Loeb and Verworn had assumed that these lowest forms were controlled only by physical and chemical laws. Loeb, it is true, admitted that the higher animals could learn from experience, in so far as later movements were different because of earlier movements. He called this associative memory, but he would deny it to the lowest animal forms. Jennings, however, showed that even the stentor would respond differently on account of the success or failure of earlier responses. After the animal had failed to get rid of a strong stimulus by contractions, he would, when it was repeated, free himself and move away. He assumed that they possess the rudiments of the capacity to learn which is characteristic of the higher animals and of man. Later he tended to emphasize the complexity rather than the simplicity of these lower forms. He always attempted, however, to give a specific explanation of each response and not to bring in purposes and consciousness. He was not willing to simplify his interpretation to the point where it would not do justice to the observed facts.

Among the theories of animal activities we find all sorts of variations. Bethe asserts that an ant is merely a physico-chemical mechanism that finds its way back to the nest along its own outgoing trail because of the setting off of certain compounds in its body through stimulation by the negatively polarized odors left on the way out. Loeb gives the higher animals a slightly more complicated mental life, in fact he analyzes up to the point where learning begins and then is content to lump it all under associative learning, with little explanation of what that means. At the upper limit are McDougall and Driesch who would make quasi-mental teleological causes effective all the way up the scale, after the manner of Aristotle and Johannes Müller. Finally we have Köhler who, more recently, would ascribe insight to apes and probably to lower animals. On the whole, it is the more mechanical theories of animal psychology that have modified the general psychological outlook. The concepts that have been taken over from it are the simple reflex and learning by trial and error, with the capacity for learning the responses that have been repeated because of their satisfying character. The effect of the law of parsimony and the denial of the right to question whether animals possess conscious states, have been highly important in all this work.

The last form of animal experimentation that has modified the conceptions of psychology is that by which the Russian physiologist Pavlov has demonstrated the existence of the conditioned reflex. Pavlov hit upon the use of the salivary reflex as a measure of the effects of

stimuli. He noticed that a dog's mouth watered as he saw food and he found it possible to use that as a measure of the possibility of transfer of response from one stimulus to another. The salivary reflex is evoked by the stimulation of the nerves of taste, and is a direct reflex through the brain stem. In his experiments Pavlov dissected out the salivary duct, and took the end out so that the saliva would drip into the scale-pan of a balance instead of within the dog's mouth. He could then record the amount secreted on a kymograph and study the conditions of the reflex. The point that has been made most of in psychology is that a connection can be formed between indifferent stimuli and the salivary reflex by simultaneous presentation of the indifferent stimulus with the stimulus which naturally induced the secretion. Thus if a bell is sounded at the same time, or a little before, the piece of meat is shown, after a score or so of repetitions the sound of the bell serves to produce a flow of saliva. This is entirely analogous to the formation of association in man, and Pavlov demonstrated that all the conditions that form the association in man tend to connect the stimuli in the dog. The transfer of the effect of the natural stimulus to an originally neutral stimulus he calls conditioning, and the term has been widely applied in recent psychological writings.

The most vigorous and aggressive of the modern schools of psychology, the behavioristic, is on one line of descent a direct outgrowth of all this work in animal psychology. As we have said, the behaviorists believe that the psychologist should study man as he studies animals. That is, he should put him in a given situation, determine the responses he makes, and draw conclusions from these responses as to what the laws of his actions are, making the best explanation he can of them. He should not attempt to obtain the aid of the man who executes the movements in interpreting them. This suggestion came from the agreement among animal psychologists not to speculate about what the animal had in mind when he performed an act. Romanes, and occasionally Hobhouse and Lloyd Morgan, had asked what important function ideas might have, even when free ideas appeared in the course of development, but the more recent workers have eliminated all reference to them, save in an occasional study. They believed that the discussion confused the issue and would lead to no useful purpose. The behaviorist applies the same principles to man.

The first man to write a completely behavioristic explanation of human action was Max Meyer, of the University of Missouri, in *The Fundamental Laws of Human Behavior*, published in 1911. In this work all psychology is restricted to a discussion of action, and action is explained as primarily reflex, with such variations as would occur owing to inaccuracy in the physiological adjustment. These accidental variations lead to hitting upon movements that are more effective in the given situation than the reflex itself. When they appear, these favorable accidents are repeated and become established as habits. Meyer attempted at once to get rid of the mental processes as such, and to transfer their functions to movements. The most characteristic and important function usually ascribed to ideas is the capacity of generalization or abstraction. This he thinks can be explained as no more than a generalized movement, a single response which can be made in the place of many single ones. If this generalized movement be at first of an external muscle, it may be symbolized by a movement of the tongue, the movements made in speech. The word heard serves as a stimulus that may take the place of the object seen which originally produced the movement. Finally the word response may serve the functions of understanding even when the appropriate movement is not evoked. Meyer insists that all the functions ordinarily studied by introspection and stated in terms of consciousness may just as well be described in terms of movement and nervous processes, and science would gain in clearness by the change. Meyer is of the opinion that all the years of investigation by means of introspection have produced nothing more than a few facts of association and attention. He asserts that the same amount of time devoted to studying the conditions of behavior objectively would have produced a much larger result. He would bar introspection altogether.

Two years after Meyer wrote, John B. Watson, then of Johns Hopkins, published an article in the Psychological Review, entitled *Psychology as the Behaviorist Views It,* in which he took essentially the same position, stated rather more clearly and positively. Introspection was to be eliminated from psychology altogether. Watson had worked mainly in animal psychology up to that time, and he insisted that man should be treated just as the animal is treated, to the extent of considering only what he does in a controlled situation and making no note of what the man himself observes or thinks during the experiment. In this first article Watson did not deny consciousness so specifically as he did later, but it was altogether irrelevant to the psychological experiment. He argued that the psychologist could make just as much progress if he neglected to consider consciousness and would avoid many sources of confusion that came from use of the concept. At this stage behaviorism was little more than functionalism minus introspection.

With the passage of time the denial of consciousness became more prominent. In *Psychology from the Standpoint of a Behaviorist,* published in 1919, Watson goes much farther, and in a popular book, *Behaviorism,* published in 1924, he leaves nothing of psychology but conditioned reflexes and tongue movements. He denies that consciousness has any existence at all in man as well as in animals, and describes as illusions all the phenomena usually included under it. Watson had conducted a series of experiments on the instincts and emotions of young infants between the appearance of the article in 1913 and the *Psychology* in 1919, and from them had been convinced that the hereditary element in man's action had been much exaggerated. He insists that the human infant has only three emotions, fear, anger, and sex, and only a few instincts and these relatively simple. All else is acquired. For the study of the methods of acquiring habits or transferring the few original instincts and emotions he urges that Pavlov's method is the best. He also adopts Pavlov's nomenclature entirely. He insists that all learning shall be called conditioning, and that it is due to simultaneous presentation of two stimuli, one of which is natively suited to evoke an emotion or instinct.

Fundamentally, Watson's position may be regarded as just the reverse of Hume's. Hume insisted that we could know only impressions and ideas, while the nature of things and any possible cause of ideas is forever hidden from us. Watson insists just as positively that the nature of ideas and of consciousness is completely hidden and that we know only things. We appreciate other men only in so far as we can observe their movements and forms of expression. We know ourselves not at all. In logic, Hume has the advantage of taking his primary reality nearer the knower, although if we grant Watson's assumption that the knower does not exist, even that logical advantage disappears. Watson would probably argue that in our common sense attitude we are working always with things and never care to consider how we know them. We are interested only in manipulating them. He certainly asserts that we can take that attitude towards people, and ask not how they know, or how we know them, but merely formulate the laws of their action as we do those of physical things and of other animals. Both Hume and Watson entirely neglect the problem of knowledge. Hume neglects it because we can never come into contact with the cause of impressions and so do not know whether they exist or not. Watson assumes that things as seen are the only reality but entirely omits to consider how we come into contact with them, or even the problem of perception as an occasion for the behavior of the people who are observed.

Watson is not quite consistent on this point, for through old habit or by oversight he is led to consider the influence of abstraction. He is not content merely to assume generalized habits, but seeks to find something that may be retained and make possible delayed responses of a general character. Language is, of course, the form that this generalized knowledge takes most frequently in the discussion of the older philosopher and psychologist. Watson follows Stricker in insisting that language is recalled always as a slight movement of the vocal organs, what he calls sub-vocal responses.

These are so slight as not to be appreciated by the outside observer, but are still sufficient to be apparent to the speaker, or at least are in some way effective. This phase of the theory seems to be, on Watson's part, the retention of a language habit from the time before he became a behaviorist. It is very hard to see how he could be interested in these movements in the light of his present theory. Even if these movements were present, they could not be appreciated without consciousness, and they are given no specific function in the control of behavior. He does not show how a slight tongue movement, if it existed, could be the occasion for a voluntary decision or its behavioristic counterpart. Behavior is controlled only through the same neural coördinations that produce these vocal responses as a by-product. They have not been demonstrated objectively by any of the careful workers who have looked for them, and if they were present could add nothing to the complicated neural coördinations that must produce them with the behavior itself. Were there consciousness they would constitute an interesting means of coloring it, but without consciousness they are futile.

A similar hold-over from the pre-behavioristic type of thinking seems to be present in the discussion of the emotions as well. They, too, are defined as masses of internal muscles in a state of contraction, or as the effects of the secretions of ductless glands. These contractions and glandular secretions, again, would have no value unless appreciated and they cannot be appreciated without consciousness. The overt responses that are seen by the outsider in the facial expression have been shown by recent work to be somewhat ambiguous. The unseen contractions of unstriped and striped muscles have no functions in themselves and no attempt has been made to show that they directly modify behavior. More could be made of the glandular secretions, but even with them the same response seems to be evoked by different types of emotions and by what would be called very different situations. To a man with consciousness they have a meaning; they might modify his behavior. To a man without consciousness they are without value, or at least no effort has been made to show what function they would have.

One statement made by Watson which seems to have no bearing on the general theory, is that all responses are acquired, that nothing can be referred to instinct or heredity. This point is one on which he has shifted his position. When the first book, *Psychology*, was published, he held that habit is largely reducible to hereditary connections. He asserts that an animal or man can make use only of synapses that are potentially open at birth. The partly or potentially open paths become fully opened in learning. In 1919, after the work on young children, he restricts the influence of heredity greatly. And finally in *Behaviorism* and later writings, he flatly states that heredity contributes nothing at all, that the child of the least intelligent parents has as good a chance in the world as the child of the greatest genius. Racial instincts have also been all but abandoned in the theory. This is of course a matter of fact and as such will some day be definitely settled. The facts at present known seem to be decidedly and definitely settled against Watson. Meantime the question is entirely apart from the essential theory of behaviorism and need not be confused with it.

Behaviorism seems to be an entirely new movement in the history of psychology. Some would suggest that it was a form of materialism, in so far as it explains all human action in physiological, if not in chemical and physical, terms. However, it does not fall in the same class as the materialisms, for they merely explain mind as a form of matter, they do not reject it. The atomists explained mind as composed of very fine particles that were found in between the cruder bodily atoms. Büchner, the mid-eighteenth century physiological materialist, said that the brain secretes thought as the liver secretes bile. Consciousness is very real for him, more solid than for the idealist. Behaviorism denies the existence of consciousness altogether. While on the extreme left among psychological schools, it is, therefore, not materialistic in the old sense. Possibly one could give a definition of materialism that would include it.

Behaviorism has had an important effect in stimulating work on man by methods similar to Pavlov's work on animals, although the net result is to show that the salivary reflex in the child can be conditioned, and somewhat less certainly that the pupillary reflex in man can be transferred. It has encouraged the work on animals, although it is hard to say whether that would not have gone on almost as well on the older theories.

The main disadvantage in the theory is that it greatly limits the field for psychology. Most of the work on perception, if not that on sensation, would be discarded unless some means can be found of devising a figure of speech that can attach the results attained so far to motor responses. It has nothing to say of imagery, of thought or imagination, or of the higher voluntary processes. One might of course make an exception of the thought process in so far as it is referred to sub-vocal speech, but nothing is made of this after it has been mentioned. There is no attempt made to develop rules for thinking or even to relate the sub-vocal response to behavior. If the behavioristic theory is retained it means that we must have two psychologies, an external and an internal, a psychology viewed from the outside and one viewed from the inside. This seems at the best an unnecessary complication.

A returning Hume would ask, where does it all lead? Each man is aware of the acts of every other man, but he knows not how he knows. Each man exists only in the knowledge of some other, and that other exists only in the awareness of the first and of some third. The stimulus is seen to affect a sense organ, and a movement results. That is known only by some one else, and we are forbidden to ask how the stimulus offered by the sight of the other man's act is appreciated by the onlooker. That could be known by the third man. Knowledge, from this point of view, goes through an endless circle but never arrives at its goal. In short, this system explains action perfectly, or would do so, did it accumulate sufficient knowledge, but it does not approach the problem that has always been central in the history of psychology, the problem of knowing. It assumes the process, but does not attempt to solve it. A mere denial of mental states does not warrant neglect of the function that they have always been assumed to perform.

CHAPTER XVIII

HORMIC PSYCHOLOGY, THE GESTALT SCHOOL, AND INTUITIONISM

THERE is a fourth among the more conservative schools that would make mental life the expression of a conscious will. It has several representatives each of whom starts with slightly different fundamental assumptions, though they are alike in that they advance the idea of some more or less substantial or actual force upon which mental processes depend and which determines their nature and course. There is a difference of opinion as to what this force is and how it acts. One group revives for the purpose the Aristotelian conception of mind as the form or entelechy of the body. As we have seen, mind for Aristotle was little more than a certain aspect of the individual which provided a control or direction of the whole. In one aspect it was the characteristic that led the organism to foreseen ends. For Aristotle himself form and matter were different phases of the same organism, but were not different things. Form was merely the characteristic of the organism, thought of as seeking an end, and not a driving force that could be separated from that organism or even from the matter of the organism. It was an urge of the type that man experiences when he feels himself active, knows what he is to do, and is willing to take the responsibility for it. It was the intelligent, teleological phase of the organic whole. In history it has been very difficult to prevent this notion from being changed into a separate self or soul. St. Thomas and many others did this, as we have seen. Attempts have been made to revive the notion of entelechy in recent times. Johannes Müller did it specifically in his vitalism, and Driesch and Bergson, among contemporary philosophies, represent the movement.

Among living psychologists, William McDougall best represents the position of this school. He has designated the theory as the hormic psychology, which he takes to mean the psychology of the individual as a goal-seeker, the purposive psychology. Attempt is made to make the purpose the characteristic dominating Aristotle's entelechy. The ends are thought of as controlling the activities not merely of man but of animals as well. It is in this sense that Aristotle ascribes form, or the nutritive and sensitive types of soul, to animals. The use of the word in this strictly Aristotelian sense is more frequent in McDougall's *Body and Mind*, where the doctrine was first stated, than in his later more popular writings. This may be no more than an expression of the general tendency for a word, once carefully defined, to become changed to a simpler, less technical use.

This is an instance of the universal tendency which we have seen all through history for a function to become a faculty, and this occurs in spite of the fact that the author himself has no intention of making the change. Whatever the cause, McDougall tends more and more to speak as if the entelechy were a separate will and not merely a function.

In his later formulations of the doctrine McDougall tends to replace entelechy by the word conation, which implies a striving. He uses it as if it were a separate driving force rather than a mere current in the stream of experience or some other phase of the entire organic activity. The force is not at all mechanical, yet it is a real, effective force and not a pale, fruitless accompaniment of organic activity. It is at once psychic and dynamic. It is not at all dependent upon the physical brain states. On the contrary, it is a psychic organization of all experience. This conation is the basis of all the general mental functions. Pleasure, e. g., in the aesthetic form, depends upon the organization of wide ranges of experience, but not upon the organism, nor even directly upon the sensory content. "This synthesis and the unitary whole and the resulting pleasurable feeling-tone of consciousness are purely psychic facts that have no immediate correlates among the brain processes." [1] Meanings, too, are supra-sensuous and supra-organic processes. They result from the organization of experiences, but

[1] Body and Mind, p. 317.

are purely psychic results of conative organizations. "Meanings are essential links between sense impressions and the behavior they evoke; not the sensations, nor any aggregate or synthesis of them, nor yet the physical correlates in the brain of the sensory contents of consciousness, but these products in consciousness of a purely psychic activity are the factors which awaken within us the appropriate emotion and stir up the impulse to the appropriate action, that psychic impulse or conation without which no action is initiated or sustained." [1] This represents the nearest approach to an independent mental entity that we have left in modern psychology. It may be emphasized again that the theory began in an attempt to develop Aristotle's notion of form or entelechy in a way to make it conform to the needs of modern science. Entelechy has been gradually transformed until it seems to be a soul. One cannot determine from the context whether the transformation was intended or whether it has come from an unfortunate use of language, or whether it is just the result of the tendency so frequently referred to to make a thing of any function. It vies with the Gestalt theory, for the position on the extreme right of modern psychology.

To Germany we must turn for two schools that are marked by an anti-analytic, and in one case by an antiscientific, tendency. Kant, it will be recalled, insisted that man cannot measure mental processes and hence

[1] Body and Mind, p. 311.

cannot develop a science of psychology. The recent movements in German psychology have tended to emphasize this fact and to seek some other method than analysis and relation of events to causes in the treatment of mental life. We have a foreshadowing of one of the movements in Münsterberg's distinction between the science of values and the science of causes or of measurements. There are a number of movements of somewhat the same general character of which we may mention two.

Possibly the most thriving, and certainly the one which has added most to our experimental and factual knowledge, is known as the Gestalt psychology. The word Gestalt means in German form or figure, but is given such a technical meaning by the school that it is as well not to translate it. The adherents of this school have occasionally been called the configurationists, but the name is awkward and carries some suggestions that are not in harmony with the teachings of the school. In one of its phases, the school may be regarded as an outgrowth of the Külpe or Würzburg doctrines, although its members would not regard themselves as descendants. Wertheimer, who first suggested the present application of the word and has been among the most aggressive in developing the doctrine, was a student of Külpe, as was Koffka, another prominent exponent of the theory. The main seat of the movement is the Psychological Institute at the University of Berlin where its workers are busily engaged on experiments which have a more or less direct bearing upon the tenets of the school. Its most important point of contact with the Würzburg school lies in the similarity between the notion of image-less thought and the belief of the Gestaltists that the essentials of perception and thought are to be found in something other than the conscious elements, a something which both leave indefinite.

Wertheimer first hit upon the idea in a study of the visual perception of movement published in 1912. Wertheimer was engaged in determining the condition under which apparent movement of lines could be produced. He would show one line for an instant in one place, and then, after an interval, another line in a nearby place. If the interval were too short, one would seem to see two lines simultaneously near together; if the interval were much longer, one would see first one line in one place, then the second in another; with a suitable intermediate interval, the first line seemed to move over to the position of the second. Wertheimer found that not merely the length of time interval and the distance of one line from the other, determined whether the line seemed to move, but that other slight factors were effective in deciding the appearance. The whole situation must be taken into account. This series of factors or the entire configuration he called the Gestalt, and the term has been generally accepted and extended to numerous other cases, in which the perception depends upon the whole rather than upon the elements.

Other workers in almost all fields of visual perception have applied the same principles and the same word. Here the assumption is that certain forms exist in the very nature of things, which are immediately recognized as wholes. These are seen in addition to and as dominating the parts which we usually think of as composing them. In a simple illustration Köhler suggests that if a series of vertical lines are drawn at even distances apart, each tends to form a single figure. If now, a second line is drawn to the right of each line and nearer it than to the next, we have a new figure composed of two lines, and these two seem marked off as distinct from the others on either side. It is said by the members of this school that instead of having two lines side by side, we have a figure that determines the way the lines shall be seen. The most characteristic statement of the school is that these figures are seen for themselves, and that they give the percept its character. There is something more than one line added to the other, and this something more constitutes the Gestalt or figure. The fundamental doctrine of the school is that these wholes determine the parts and are not merely constituted of the parts.

It follows from this that we have no right to divide an experience into its elements, for the elements are not essential to the inner being of the experience. To divide may destroy the spirit. The parts do not by summa-

tion give the whole, so that it is relatively useless to enumerate them. Elements when discovered would be merely introducing new figures or new Gestalten, they would not be analyzing the whole. It follows also that the laws of association are relatively unimportant. When two sensations combine, not the laws of combination but the Gestalt gives life or meaning to the new creation, and that meaning was present before the elements were combined. The parts are not held together by any cohesion between them as units, but by the effect of the over-figure of Gestalt that was present in mind before they were and before they combined. Possibly it would be safer to say that we should raise no question of what brings the parts back or holds them together, for it is the whole that we are interested in and this is given with relatively little relation to what we call the units or parts. Nothing remains that is similar to the ordinary explanation. One can only enumerate the Gestalten or wholes.

The notion of Gestalt is reminiscent of several other ways of representing the meaning of an idea or group of ideas. It is not unlike the original Aristotelian form that gives unity or effectiveness to the body. It is the determiner of the meaning of the parts and in a sense holds them together and makes them effective. It strikes the beholder as the essence of the experience. Gestalt also bears a resemblance to the Würzburg imageless thought, in so far as it is the meaning with little or no embodiment in the images or elements. It is relatively independent of sensory experience. Even when the sensory elements are taken into account, they are mere concomitants of the Gestalt, not really determinants of it. Understanding lies in the form alone and the elements are merely chance factors subordinate to it.

Exactly where the Gestalten come from or how they are acquired is not altogether a matter of agreement. On the whole they seem to be given in advance of experience and not acquired through it. Gottschaldt, for example, in two long investigations demonstrated that giving separate parts of a complicated figure several hundred times in advance of showing the figure itself did not permit the observer to recognize the part in the whole. In the experiments, each part shown usually had a definite meaning or Gestalt of its own and cut across two or more parts of the composite or complicated figure. This to some extent accounts for the difficulty in recognizing the parts in the whole. Gottschaldt argues that the experiments prove that a Gestalt cannot be developed through experience. In certain instances, Köhler speaks as if certain combinations or nonsense syllables, which are frequently repeated together, become a Gestalt. This would be a case of an acquired or developed Gestalt. Köhler seems in general to assume that the wholes are given in advance of experience, although they may be amplified or developed by use. He asserts that there has been a great tendency in the study of perception to make too much of the influence of experience, that most of perception is innate. On the whole then, it seems that the members would agree that a Gestalt is for the most part an inborn figure or disposition to see a figure into which the sensory elements fit. Whether innate or not, the Gestalt is a natural unit; it is an easy and even necessary way of interpreting single sensory components. We cannot avoid using it.

Gestalten are not all on the same level. Some are said to be good or natural Gestalten, others poor; some are complete, others are incomplete. The more fully developed or more natural are said to be the better, as are the more readily recognized and the more clear-cut. Open and closed Gestalten are also recognized. These can be tested empirically. Draw a horizontal base line and then draw upward from each end other lines at acute angles, but which do not meet to form the apex of the triangle. This is an open Gestalt, and there is always a tendency to close it. If it is shown for a very brief interval or in a very dim light, the gap at the top will not be seen. The same may be said of a circle with a gap in it. In a faint light or with a very brief exposure the gap will not be noticed. A closed or good Gestalt will replace the open or poor one.

The Gestalten are the basis of explanation of all mental processes. Thinking depends upon the application of correct Gestalten to the empirical data. Give a student a problem in geometry and he may look at it for a long time without result, then suddenly he sees it in the right light and the solution comes at once. Seeing in the right light constitutes applying the correct Gestalt. The presence of the Gestalt and its correct application constitute the conditions for correct thinking.

Explanation of the more active phases of mental life in terms of the principle has been undertaken. In this the general premises of the purposive psychology have been accepted and developed in a new way. The main difference is that the word Gestalt has been substituted for aim. First signs of a Gestalt are found in what is ordinarily called instinctive action, since it is noted that the response depends upon the wider situation instead of merely upon the stimulus. A bit of filth causes the ape to make a movement of withdrawal with a look of disgust if it is on his hand or foot, but is eaten at once if it is in his mouth. In explaining learning the Gestaltists insist that the method of trial and error is not truly descriptive or explanatory. Animals do not learn merely by repeating chance movements until they hit upon a satisfactory result. On the contrary, from the beginning, they act with a series of definite movements apparently adapted to the appropriate end, and a single movement suffices to bring success. Köhler cites frequent incidents in his studies of apes in which problems seem to be solved in a flash, as if the animals had thought the problem through in advance and then applied their conclusions. Thus, when a banana was put at a distance from the cage too great to be reached by hand or by any piece of bamboo in sight, and the ape was given two pieces of bamboo, one smaller than the other, he would place the smaller in the larger, thus increasing the length and pull the fruit towards him with it. Acts of this kind are said to be due to insight, and the implication is that the insight is an application of a Gestalt. It is interesting to note that Hobhouse in his *Mind in Evolution*, published in 1901, uses the term "articulate ideas" to describe or explain similar accomplishments on the part of monkeys and dogs.

Lewin in particular has advanced the suggestion that all movements, from the so-called instincts up, can be explained in terms of the dynamic effects of Gestalten. On this assumption, each unit can be said to have a force that is either positive or negative, and in accordance with its sign would tend to cause a movement towards or away from a given object. A child tends to draw towards certain objects as soon as they are presented, and to move away from others just as immediately. It is suggested that certain of the Gestalten are to be regarded as initiating the movements on the basis of positive and negative forces which attach to them in connection with the objects involved.

The Gestalt school has brought together many of the synthetic aspects of different earlier psychological theories, which had been interpreted in different ways by those other theories. As we have noticed, it is like the

Külpe school in finding the significance of mental contact in something other than the content itself. While the Külpe school is content to speak of thought without images, the Gestalt school designates thought in a slightly different way as the whole situation or something that depends upon the whole. Like the Külpe school, too, it is dissatisfied with the explanation offered by associations. Instead, however, of being content to supplement associationism by giving the associative connections the additional control of attitudes, it replaces the whole notion by the statement that one should consider not the elements which may be associated, but larger wholes which do not need to be analyzed. It makes the units much greater and thus avoids the necessity of seeing how they are put together. The Gestalt as something significant apart from the image is also reminiscent of the notion of meaning, as it is developed in the neo-Hegelian logicians, Bradley and Bosanquet. The dominance of purpose relates it to Mc-Dougall. The insistence that all mental processes are understood with reference to innate fixed mental units is reminiscent of the Platonic ideas, or at least of the Kantian forms and categories.

It should be said that the exponents of the theory are not willing to admit that any one of these earlier or similar doctrines is like their own in any important or essential respect. When G. E. Müller, for example, suggested that the notion of Gestalt added nothing strikingly different from the notions of complexes that he had developed in connection with his study of memory, and those of attitude that had been made so much of by Külpe and Ach, Köhler replied very bitterly that there was little or no connection between the two ideas, and that Müller had failed to understand the Gestalt.

A final judgment on the Gestaltists cannot yet be passed. Theoretically they have brought together a large number of facts which cannot be brought under the simpler psychological laws. They have raised a number of important problems. Whether the suggestions they offer for the solution of these problems are more satisfactory than a combination of those supplied by other schools is yet a question. They deserve great credit for the large amount of experimental work they have conducted in the development of their theories, and which have great value apart from the particular interpretation they give them. In general, they do not reject any of the phenomena that have been investigated by others; all they do is to rewrite the older psychology in new terms. In their nomenclature they deal always with units as whole and should name these wholes and not attempt to analyze them into their elements. It is a weakness of the school that they have not been able more definitely to describe Gestalten, or even to enumerate them. We are to believe that everything depends upon them, that they alone serve any useful purpose, but, so far, the school has gone little further than to insist that these Gestalten alone have any value for explanation, without saying what they are or how they act.

Even more in revolt against the traditional methods of psychology, and still more inclined to find all explanation in the vague and indefinite, is the work of the so-called Understanding School of psychology, represented by Spranger, Binswanger and Ewald. Spranger is Professor of Education at the University of Berlin, Binswanger is a psychiatrist and head of a private sanitarium, Ewald is assistant Professor of Psychiatry at the University of Erlangen. In one respect this group holds a position resembling Münsterberg's psychology of values. Like him they would divide psychology into two parts: the explanatory psychology which seeks out the causal relations, and the understanding psychology which classifies men and mental phenomena according to types. The word they apply to their method is apparently taken from Dilthey's aphorism, "We explain nature; we understand man." For Spranger the process of understanding seems to consist in dividing man's purposes with reference to their aesthetic, their religious, their social, their economic, their theoretical, and their dynamic values. The questions are applied to the psychophysical, to the lower mental processes, and to the higher soul processes. So far the analysis has not gone much farther than to outline a program and cannot be judged by its results, in spite of several volumes devoted to its exposition. It is to be regarded as one of several signs of a tendency in Germany to abandon the attempt to explain by detailed analysis and reference to causes, and to seek to develop a psychology by the enumeration and classification of the various affective and "value" phases of mental life. It must be judged by its own standards, for it cannot be brought under the categories of the schools which we have found in history.

The enumeration and description of the present day schools show that there is no lack of variety of opinion. If in the world of scientific theory, as in the evolution of living species, the appearance of a great number of "sports" is the necessary antecedent of advance through the survival of the fit, psychology is in no danger of stagnation. Fortunately it is not in the province of the historian to prophecy which is likely to survive.

BIBLIOGRAPHY

GENERAL

Baldwin: *History of Psychology* (New York, 1915).
Brett: *History of Psychology*, 3 vols. (London; New York, 1912–21).
Dessoir: *History of Psychology* (New York, 1912).
Dessoir: *Geschichte der neueren deutschen Psychologie* (Berlin, 1912).
Klemm: *History of Psychology* (New York, 1914).
Murphy: *Introduction to Modern Psychology* (New York, 1929).
Warren: *History of Association Psychology* (New York, 1920).

CHAPTER I

Burnet: *Early Greek Philosophers* (London).
Burnet: *Greek Philosophy* (New York, 1920).
Chaignet: *Histoire de la psychologie des Grecs* (Paris, 1887–1893).
Jowett: *The Dialogues of Plato* (New York, 1885–1893).
Hammond: *Aristotle's Psychology* (New York, 1902).
Gomperz: *Greek Thinkers* (New York, 1901–12).

CHAPTER II

Pagel: *Geschichte der Medizin*, 1898.
Neuburger-Pagel: *Handbuch der Geschichte der Medizin.* Vol. I, 1901.
St. Augustine: *Confessions* (London, 1909).
St. Thomas: *Summa Theologica.*

Chapter III

Kuno Fischer: *Geschichte der neueren Philosophie.* Vol. i, ii, 1893.
    ibid: *History of Philosophy.* Vol. i (New York, 1887).
Joachim: *Study of Spinoza's Ethics* (Oxford, 1905).
Mahaffy: *Descartes* (London, 1887).

Chapter IV

Fraser, A. C.: *Locke* (London, 1890).
Morley: *Locke* (New York, 1880).
Tönnies: *Hobbes* (Stuttgart, 1896).
Leslie Stephen: *Hobbes* (New York, 1904).
A. E. Taylor: *Hobbes* (1908).
Merz: *Leibniz* (London, 1884).
Bertrand Russell: *The Philosophy of Leibniz* (Cambridge, 1900).

Chapter V

Fraser: *Berkeley* (Oxford, 1881).
Huxley: *Hume* (New York, 1902).
Bower: *Hartley and Mill* (London, 1881).
Ribot: *English Psychology* (New York, 1874).
Offner: *Die Psychologie Bonnet,* 1893.

Chapter VI

Dessoir: *Geschichte der neueren deutschen Psychologie* (Berlin, 1894).
Meyer: *Kant's Psychology* (1870).
Uebele: *Tetens* (Kant Studien: Ergänzundsht, 1911).

Chapter VII

McCosh: *Scottish Philosophy* (New York, 1875).
Mill, J. S.: *Examination of Sir William Hamilton* (New York, 1873).
Mill, J. S.: *Autobiography* (London, 1875).
Bower: *Mill and Hartley* (London, 1871).

318   BIBLIOGRAPHY

Chapter VIII

Elsenhans: *Fries und Kant* (1906).
Davidson: *New Interpretation of Herbart's Psychology.*
Herbart: *Text-book of Psychology* (New York, 1891).
Ribot: *German Psychology of To-day* (New York, 1887).

Chapter IX

Johannes Müller: *Elements of Physiology* Tr. by W. Baly
    (London, 1838).
Pagel und Neuburger: *Handbuch der Geschichte der Medi-
    zin,* vol. ii, 1903.
Königsberger: *Hermann von Helmholtz* (Oxford, 1906).

Chapter X

Lasswitz: *Fechmer* (Stuttgart, 1896).
G. Stanley Hall: *Founders of Modern Psychology.*
Cattell: *On Feelings and Emotions* (Worcester: Wittenberg
    Volume, 1928), pp. 427–438.
Ribot: *German Psychology of To-day* (New York,1874).

Chapter XI

Spencer: *Autobiography* (New York, 1904).
Bain: *Autobiography* (New York, 1904).
Bettany: *Life of Chas. Darwin* (London, 1887).
Galton: *Memories of My Life* (London, 1909)

Chapter XII

Krause: *Franz Brentano* (München: Beck, 1919).
Titchener: *Brentano and Wundt.* American Journal of Psy-
    chology, vol. 33, pp. 108–120.
Titchener: *Psychology of Act and Faculty Psychology.* Am.
    J. of Psy., vol. 33, pp. 519–542; vol. 34, pp. 43–83.
Titchener: *Experimental Psychology of the Thought Proces-
    ses* (New York, 1909),

Chapter XIII

Picavet: *Les idéologues* (Paris, 1891).

Ravaison: *La philosophie en France au xix⁰ siecle* (Paris, 1867).

Boutroux: *Philosophie en France depuis 1867, Rev. de Metaphysique et Morale,* 1908.

Th. Simon: *Alfred Binet.* L'Année psychologique, vol. 18, p. 1.

Largnier des Bancels: *L'Œuvre de Alfred Binet.* ibid., p. 16.

Chapter XIV

James: *The Letters of William James* (Boston, 1920).

Flournoy: *The Philosophy of William James* (New York, 1917).

G. Stanley Hall: *Confessions of a Psychologist* (New York, 1924).

Ruckmich: *Psychological Laboratories in America.* Am. Jour. of Psych., vol. 23, pp. 517–531.

Chapter XV

Janet: *Psychological Healing* (New York, 1920).

Janet: *The Major Symptoms of Hysteria* (New York, 1920).

Wittels: *S. Freud* (New York, 1924).

Jung: *Psychological Types* (New York, 1923).

Adler: *Practice and Theory of Individual Psychology* (New York, 1924).

Chapter XVI

Titchener: *Postulates of a Structural Psychology.* Philosophical Review, vol. 7, p. 449.

Pillsbury: *The Psychology of E. B. Titchener.* Philosophical Review, vol. 33, pp. 95–108.

Angell: *The Province of Functional Psychology.* Psychological Review, vol. 14, pp. 169–181.

CHAPTER XVII

Washburn: *Animal Psychology* (New York, 1927).
Warden: *An Outline of Comparative Psychology* (New York, 1928).
Watson: *Behaviorism* (New York, 1927).
Watson and McDougall: *The Battle of Behaviorism* (New York, 1929).

CHAPTER XVIII

McDougall: *Body and Mind* (New York, 1911).
Köhler: *Gestalt Psychology* (New York, 1929).
Köhler: *The Mentality of Apes* (New York, 1925).
Spranger: *Types of Men* (Halle, 1928).
Külver: *Appendix to Murphy's Introduction to Modern Psychology* (1929).
Proceedings: *VIIIth Congress of Psychology*, pp. 117–147, 175–197.

INDEX OF TOPICS

INDEX OF NAMES